THE GUINNESS GUIDE TO
TWENTIETH CENTURY FASHION

GUINNESS SUPERLATIVES LIMITED
2 Cecil Court, London Road, Enfield, Middlesex.

The GUINNESS Guide to

20th Century Fashion

David Bond.

DEDICATED TO MY FATHER – RICHARD BOND

Editor: Anne Marshall

© David Bond and Guinness Superlatives Limited, 1981

ISBN 0-85112-234-5

British Library CIP Data
Bond, David
The Guinness Guide to 20th Century Fashion
1. Costume design – Great Britain – 20th century
I. Title
746.9'2   TT507
ISBN 0-85112-234-5

Published by Guinness Superlatives Limited
2 Cecil Court, London Road, Enfield, Middlesex

Guinness is a registered trademark of Guinness Superlatives Limited

Design and layout: Jean Whitcombe

Typeset by Sprint, Beckenham, Kent.
Printed and bound by South China Printing Co., Hong Kong

Contents

PREFACE

Until the end of the 18th-century, fashion had been created for, and set by, the court circles. In the Middle Ages certain colours and fabrics had been restricted to the nobles, and rank and wealth were clearly shown through dress. After the French Revolution aristocrats dressed less flamboyantly; their position in society was shown by their clothes but it was no longer flaunted.

The 19th-century Industrial Revolution created the powerful middle classes, fashion began to cater for this new market and by the beginning of the 20th-century prosperous middle class and aristocratic dressing had merged into a general upper-class style.

World wars, revolutions and the rapid social changes of the last 80 years have produced more changes in the way people dressed than any comparable period in history.

In my father's lifetime he has seen women's skirts trailing the streets and so short they barely covered the seat. Breasts have been exaggerated until they looked like deformities, and bound to make them as flat as a thin man's chest. Shoulders have been padded out like Harlem Globetrotters and sloped like bottle-tops. Women's hair has been grown to waist length and swept on top of the head over false pads, less than 15 years later it was shorn like an army recruit.

Men have dressed to look affluent and reliable and to appear deliberately poor and ragged. Suede shoes have been thought effeminate and shoulder-length curls manly enough for construction workers.

Fashion, like writing, humour and music, is a social reflection; it is transitory. Clothes always suit the period and look right at the time. One could not imagine the stately Edwardian women in the skimpy fashions of the twenties, the flappers in Dior's New Look of the late forties, or the 1960s Swingers in the ethnic layers of the seventies.

The social changes of the century are mirrored by the changes in fashion, each decade unravels its own fascinating character.

Acknowledgements

I would like to thank English *Vogue*, particularly the invaluable help and assistance in collecting information from their library.

I am also grateful to the many friends and relatives who allowed me to go through their family photographs, some of which have been used to illustrate the book. My thanks also to Jill Hart who typed most of the manuscript for me.

The 1900s

Long hair was piled on top of the head, pads or false hair sometimes being added to give the admired look of fullness and weight.

The early 1900s were in many ways an extension of the 19th century, an Indian Summer for the established social order which showed little sign of being in its last few years.

Fashion started at the top with the upper classes, closely followed by the prosperous middle classes, and then gradually worked its way down the social scale. The fashions at the beginning of the new century would have held few shocks for the women of the last decades of the 19th century. Women were still rigidly corseted, clothes were as elaborate as ever and the conspicuous show of wealth and rank continued unabashed.

Women dressed in an ultra-feminine impractical way and could not have led a busy domestic or business life in their clothes. The upkeep in time and labour of the fashionable woman's wide range of outfits with undergarments, hats, shoes and gloves could only have belonged to a time where cheap domestic help was available. Ladies' maids were essential to supervise the range of clothes and help get the wearer in and out of outfits and arrange the ornate hair styles. Mass-produced clothes were unknown to these women. Hours were spent by dressmakers, seamstresses and embroiderers producing complicated, highly-decorated clothes. Like the domestic help, the labour needed to make the garments was cheap and plentiful.

The women's looks that were admired were those of the mature women with a well-rounded figure. The fashionable thinness of later decades would have horrified the Edwardians. Faces were usually round and serene, perhaps slightly haughty or languid but never angular or made-up. Prosperous fashion-conscious women followed the S-shaped silhouette. Hair was piled on top of the head often over pads to give a look of fullness and weight. Hats sat on top of the Pompadour hair styles and, although in the first half of the decade they were fairly moderate in size, they were very elaborately trimmed with ribbons, lace, flowers, feathers and veils, sometimes all on the same hat. Necks appeared very long and slender with high collars boned up to the base of the ears.

Breasts were exaggeratedly pushed forward but rather low, giving a pouter-pigeon effect. Waists were pulled in with boned and tightly laced corsets. The claims of eighteen-inch waists may have been exaggerations, and many of the fashion drawings of the period showed women with impossibly small waists, but photographs do confirm that it was pulled in as far as possible. With pulled in waists, hips appeared very curved and rounded. The extreme styles fitted the hips tightly and started to flare out from the thighs to flounce widely and trail out on the ground giving a trumpet line to the skirt and complete the fashionable S shape. A more modified version of this line was worn by many women, particularly the skirts which

At the beginning of the century, women's dress was ultra feminine and impractical – a great many garments were needed to complete each outfit.

Hats in the first half of the decade sat on top of the head. Although these 1904 styles were fairly moderate in size they were elaborately trimmed.

Figure constraining whalebone corsets were used to exaggerate every curve of the female form.

Heavy, unrevealing clothes extended even into underslips and nightdresses.

were cut full from the waist, flowing gradually to greater fullness at the hem rather than the tight hip-fitting of the more extreme S-shape styles.

Women wore a great many garments to complete even one outfit. Confining corsets were designed to exaggerate every curve of the female form. Apart from a brief period at the beginning of the previous century, tightly-laced corsets had been worn for several hundred years and were considered a permanent basic requirement in achieving a fashionable figure. As well as corsets, many underclothes were worn — long knickers, underslips and several petticoats. They were intricately made garments in cotton, lace or embroidered silk and were often finely pleated or tucked and trimmed with ribbons. Over the corsets and the underclothes, dresses were even more elaborate. Shoulder cape effects in lace or flimsy materials, pleated or frilled, were added to some dresses and many styles had extra layers of fabrics forming oversleeves and overskirts. The only areas of flesh shown were the face and hands. These were also often covered when going out — gloves were always worn and many hats had face veils.

Fashionable women's clothes were very fussy and over-decorated by later 20th-century standards, but colours were usually soft and pretty — mauves, lilacs, grey and light blues were the popular shades. Upper-class women led busy and formal social lives, requiring many outfits and changing their clothes several times a day. In the morning what was considered a comparatively simple dress or blouse and skirt would be worn at home. A more elaborate outfit would be changed into for shopping and lunch, another for the afternoon, particularly if going out or having people to afternoon tea. Hats were kept on indoors when out to lunch or visiting. Evening dress was always worn for dinner, even if quietly at home with the family. Spring, summer, autumn and winter clothes were clearly defined. The summer season, particularly London's glittering season, needed many outstanding outfits and although it was considered bad form or vulgar to try to outshine and outdo with clothes, many women couldn't resist the opportunity to try. Hours were spent with milliners and dressmakers trying

Fashionable women's clothes were fussy and over decorated but colours were usually soft and pretty and evening dresses had daringly low necklines.

This photograph from 1902 shows the stiff figure, constraining silhouette and very covered-up dress. More cover was added with extra layers of fabric forming shoulder capes, oversleeves and overskirts.

to concoct the most impressive hats and dresses. The designs had to be exclusive. A fashion-conscious woman wouldn't have considered buying an outfit that might not be totally exclusive to her alone.

Day dresses were very covered up but evening dresses often had daringly low necklines. Rich-looking jewellery was worn in great quantities, even with day dresses. Tiaras, necklaces, particularly high rows of pearls called 'chokers', bracelets, brooches and rings were all worn, often at the same time, and were made from real precious stones. To wear false jewellery would have been considered very bad taste indeed.

Furs and fur trimming has always been a sign of opulence in dress, and few periods could rival the 1900s for its popularity. Capes and coats, short and full length, were worn by the wealthy. Ermine and sable were most sought after but fox was also popular, musquash and pony less expensive and lower in status. Foxes round the shoulders and fur ties at the neck with fur hats and matching fur muffs were much worn. A fashionable woman had several fur coats, capes and ties to complete her winter outfits as well as many cloth garments with lavish fur trimmings.

Very feminine blouses were characteristic of the period and were worn by all classes. They followed the same line as dresses with high necks and long sleeves. A great deal of work went in to producing the fine rows of pleats or tucks often used on the bodices and repeated on the sleeves and collars. Blouses were sometimes made of lace or had lace insertions or *appliqué*.

Society women's clothes, like Lady Tenterden's wedding and going-away outfit in 1906, had to be specially and exclusively designed.

Young girls embroidered evening dress with a long train attached to the bodice.

Very feminine blouses were characteristic of the
period. A great deal of work went into producing the
lace inserts and the fine rows of pleats and tucks.

Fine embroidery was also greatly used. Because the blouses tucked into the tops of skirts and
looked baggier than bodices of dresses, they were sometimes described as Russian blouses.
However, the firmly corseted figure beneath them was always fairly evident. Expensive blouses
could be easily recognised although some home dressmakers made very good attempts to
achieve the look of the top fashion houses and dressmakers, and the popularity of fussy
feminine blouses continued for many years. They were considered flattering, useful garments
that could add variety to outfits and be altered or retrimmed with fashion changes, thus
lasting longer.

During the first half of the decade, the fashion changes were variations within the
established shape and line. Colours, fabrics, trimmings and styles in hats marked the
differences in the seasons and years.

As the decade progressed, social changes that had been germinating since the later years of
the 19th century became more apparent. The more independently-minded woman who had
directly developed from the so-called 'new woman' of the 1880s and 1890s began to make her
presence felt and be taken seriously. More women were going to universities and colleges,
entering professions and participating in active sports such as cycling, tennis and golf. They
supported women's suffrage, sometimes actively with the Votes for Women campaign. Their
new attitudes were being reflected in their dress which was more practical and less fussy and
frilly than the women portrayed in the fashion plates. Tailored jackets, like a man's suit
jacket, which had been thought so unfeminine in the 1890s, became firmly established, and
although its popularity has waned from time to time, a version has been fashionable in all
20th-century decades. The tailored jacket was still very figure fitting but less exaggeratedly so

Women, increasingly becoming independent, began
to make their presence felt, often supporting the
Votes for Women campaign. These new attitudes
were reflected in the more practical style of dress.

Women still rode side saddle in long flowing skirts.

than the dresses. With it was worn a matching skirt, usually pleated for easy movement and
slightly shorter — it touched the floor but did not trail. Plainer blouses were worn with these
suits. Some women even wore high round collars and ties like a man's shirt and tie. Their
hats were also plainer with far fewer fussy trimmings. Many men of the period didn't like the
attitude of these modern women and criticised their views and appearance. One British MP
irritated many women by saying in the Houses of Parliament that if the suffragettes were all
as pretty as his wife he would give them the vote tomorrow. The tailored suit soon became
popular with most women, and, apart from being more practical it could possess great style

Many more women participated in active sports, such as cycling.

Many men objected to the new 'modern' women and criticised their appearance in caps, collars and ties.

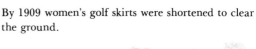

By 1909 women's golf skirts were shortened to clear the ground.

and elegance, especially summer suits in beiges and creams worn with large flattering hats draped with veiling.

Liberal attitudes were spreading in the artistic and intellectual world and this was reflected in dress. The more *avant-garde* women began to wear dresses with flowing lines rather than the stiffer corseted ones. Classical styles began to be admired and influence newer flowing dresses, particularly for the evening. By the middle of the decade quite conservative women's magazines such as the *Lady's Field* were showing evening dresses with classical lines, still waisted but less rigidly so and often indicating a high waisted effect. 'Directoire' was a popular way of describing the new styles. During the second half of the decade classical or Directoire influences were much discussed and promoted but they had a very limited effect on many women who thought them too extreme or too arty. Tight-laced corsets and covered up clothes had been established for many generations and it was difficult for many women to accept a totally different concept of dress.

Important fashion changes are often credited to the ideas of one designer, although they are usually part of a general movement in similar new ideas. However, certain designers do seem to capture the mood or spirit of the period particularly well. Paul Poiret was one of these designers. He was in his twenties during the 1900s and had worked as an assistant designer for two famous Paris fashion houses of the time, Doucet and Worth. Like many creative designers with advanced ideas he became frustrated with the limitations of working for established couture houses and started up on his own. After a few years of gradually building a reputation as an interesting and advanced designer, he launched his revolutionary ideas. He was one of the first of the 20th-century designers to have his own vision of how he wanted women to look rather than designing variations within the established shape and lines.

The clothes he designed were far less corseted. They showed a younger lithe form. Poiret claimed rather dramatically to have freed women from 'the tyranny of the corset'. His designs certainly showed more of the natural shape of the figure. Waists were high and loosely marked, rather like the styles of the first decade of the 19th century. The shape of the thighs

In the second half of the decade the basic silhouette began to change. These two drawings from 1906 (right) and 1909 show how the line was gradually becoming slimmer and straighter with wider, deeper sitting hats.

An early Paul Poiret design in 1908. His revolutionary new concept in fashion was for less corseted clothes that showed a younger lithe form.

and legs showed clearly – this was very daring for the time. A fashion showing the full length and shape of women's legs had not been seen for 100 years. His designs were often called 'Directoire' to fit in with the general interest and revival in that period but Poiret was also inspired by ancient Egypt, Greece and Rome as well as the more exotic traditional styles of the Middle East, the Orient and Russia. In fact, some of his more extreme outfits verged on the fancy-dress or stage costume and were thought outrageous by some women. When his designs were shown for the first time in London in 1908, a society figure of the period burst into laughter during the showing of his collection and called the new styles ridiculous. 'Madame', Poiret replied, 'if you wish to see old-fashioned clothes kindly continue to frequent English Houses. I do not cater for elderly ladies from the provinces.'

His controversial and revolutionary ideas were to have a lasting influence on fashion. Some of the younger women of the time, wanting to shock their Victorian elders, quickly took up the new styles with their looser bodices and very narrow hobble skirts two or three years before they were generally worn.

Poiret also helped popularise the wearing of scarves and turbans around the hair, either in a fabric or colour that matched or cleverly contrasted with the dress. For evening very oriental-looking turbans were sometimes worn with a feather or groups of feathers and jewels decorating the front. Poiret used strong vivid colours for many of his designs, adding to the theatrical look.

The 1900s were in many ways a confident and progressive decade. Technical developments were affecting everyday life. The telephone and electric light were becoming more commonplace; people travelled more; flying caught the imagination although it was still in its early stages; motor transport was increasing every year and speeding up day-to-day life. Society absorbed the accelerating pace of change but it was bound to affect clothes and introduce a more practical style of dress, if somewhat slowly at first. From 1907 onwards the basic silhouette did change. The line became slimmer and straighter, less tightly-waisted and with a growing tendency for a high-waisted effect. Comparing fashion illustrations in *Weldon's Journal*, a middle-level woman's magazine of the time for dressmakers, the change

By the late 1900s hats had become larger and even more lavishly trimmed. Humerous magazines were full of cartoons pointing out the foolishness and dangers of fashionable hats, both to the wearer and the general public.

of line shows between the illustrations of 1906 and 1909. Skirts were definitely less full and trailing. Feet sometimes showed but never ankles.

As the silhouette became slimmer and straighter, hats got larger and larger, hair was now worn rather lower and less padded in the front. The newer styles were fuller at the sides and back, following the classical influence. Hats sat deeper on the head with deep crowns and very wide brims. They were more lavishly trimmed than ever. Feathers were very popular, often sticking out beyond the brim or curling round the brim and almost touching the shoulders. Some of these hats were called 'Merry Widow' hats, and were influenced by the popular Merry Widow operetta of the time. By 1908 and 1909 hats had become amazing in size and decoration, making it one of the most hat-conscious periods. With these very large hats topping the slim, straighter line the silhouette had become more like the letter T than the S shape of the early years of the decade. Newspapers and magazines made comments pointing out the dangers and foolishness of the fashionable hats, both to the wearer and the general public. Humorous magazines such as *Punch* and *London Opinion* were also full of quips and cartoons.

Feet rarely showed under long trailing skirts, shoes were neat, elegant designs that complemented the outfit in quietly toning colours.

Setting out for a picnic. The girl on the left, although well in her teens, is not yet old enough to have her hair 'up' and wear long dresses. The young men are in their summer boaters.

Perhaps because women's legs were never shown and feet were only partly seen when sitting down, stockings and shoes were not given much attention. The well-off wore silk stockings in dark colours, and handmade shoes and boots with fairly pointed toes and only moderately high heels. Heel shapes were curved and known as 'Louis' heels. Silk or fine kid was used for the more dressy styles which sometimes had small buckles or silk bows decorating the front. Shoes were neat and elegant and complemented the outfit in matching or quietly toning colours. Everyday shoes were quite practical. Many were laced up styles with almond-shaped toes and Cuban or Louis heels. Similar styles were worn in the summer in light-coloured kid or canvas-type fabrics with matching pale-coloured stockings. Calf high-buttoned boots with the same shaped toes and heels were sometimes worn in the winter. Some styles had attached fabric tops like men's spats of the period and were in basic colours such as beige and grey.

Fashionable women needed many pairs of gloves. They were always worn with outdoor clothes – summer and winter. Everyday styles were usually in washable kid. Beautifully-made expensive gloves were sometimes in finely-embroidered suede or silk; they had small buttons at the wrists so that they could fit tightly over the lower arms. Elbow or upper-arm length gloves were quite often worn with afternoon and evening dresses.

Very few handbags were shown in the fashion illustrations of the 1900s; when they did appear they were small and decorative and hung on delicate straps from the wrists. There was not much need for larger bags – cosmetics were not used and many middle- and upper-class women charged items from the shops to their accounts and had them delivered to their

Special outfits were introduced for motoring. Most cars were open and many country roads dusty and muddy. Motoring hats had thick veils and were often worn with goggles.

Men's jackets and coats were cut on straightish lines, trousers were narrow in the leg but not very tightly fitting around the seat giving a slightly peg top effect.

Upper-class men needed clothes for many different occasions. High-standing collars and frock coats were worn for all formal occasions and for everyday business life by many professional men.

homes. Thus hands were free from large bags and parcels and more feminine accessories were carried. Fur muffs completed many winter outfits. In the summer, parasols trimmed with frills or lace were matched to afternoon dresses. In the evenings, fans were held and although they were not as coyly used as they had been by Victorian women, they still gave shy or nervous women something to do with their hands.

Men were very clothes conscious during the 1900s. The dandy revival of the 1890s continued, although perhaps in a less effete way. To be correctly dressed was very important and the English gentleman was the ideal. Paris led women's fashions but London set the style for men's clothes, and those who could afford it came to London to have their suits, shirts and shoes made. Like the women of the period upper-class men needed clothes for many different occasions and times of the day and a servant to look after them. Top hats and cutaway or double-breasted long frockcoats were worn for all formal occasions and for everyday business life by many professional men. Less formal were the basic suits consisting of jacket, waistcoat and trousers. Waistcoats were worn even with summer suits and shirts with ties were always worn. Collars were still rather high and curved at the front. They turned over as they still do today, but with more formal outfits and for evening a stand-up collar band was worn and sometimes a silk stock instead of a tie. Jackets were cut on straightish lines with high fastening, small collars and revers. Braiding was sometimes used, particularly tone-on-tone effects, dark grey on a light grey suit, or brown on a beige suit. Check suits were also sometimes braided in a toning colour. Trousers were cut narrow in the leg but not very tightly fitting around the thighs and seat, giving a slightly peg-top look with the straight line of the jacket.

Although shoes were gaining in popularity, boots laced up to or just above the ankle were still greatly worn, always highly polished. Buttoned cloth spats were also popular over shoes or boots.

Headgear was worn or at least carried with all outfits, certain styles being considered correct for certain occasions or types of outfits. Top hats were always worn with formal clothes. With everyday suits a Homburg, a hat with a slightly-curved brim and a dent in the crown, or bowlers were worn. Deerstalkers, tweed hats, sometimes trimmed with feathers, and more basic caps were worn for sportswear and in the country. Straw hats were often worn in the summer – boaters being very popular, particularly with the younger generation. A side- or forward-tilted boater was thought rather dashing and some young men wore them with dinner jackets, giving a slightly rakish look to a rather sober and formal outfit.

Apart from small neat moustaches and an occasional rather academic looking van Dyke beard, men favoured a clean-shaven appearance. Side whiskers, heavy moustaches or shaggy beards were very much the look of the older generation. Hair was short and neat, usually fairly flat with either a side or centre parting, helping to give an athletic, manly look. Men were becoming more conformist in their style of dress and the scope for the individualist was narrowing. The quickening pace of life and the new radical attitudes of the time although beginning to be reflected in women's clothes were not so much in men's. Even the free-thinking writers and social reformers conformed to the style of the English gentleman.

Wearing distinctly different types of clothes for special occasions gave men the opportunity to dress up and change their appearance. Country weekend parties were popular with the upper classes who enjoyed plenty of riding and shooting. For shooting, or even general country wear, heavy tweeds in checks or herringbone were used for capes, Norfolk jackets and knickerbockers. With knickerbockers thick woollen socks and lace-up ankle boots were worn or gaiters buttoning up the calf. In the summer, blazers and cream-coloured flannel trousers were worn with light-coloured felt or straw hats. For yachting, double-breasted, brass-buttoned, naval style jackets and peak caps gave the correct nautical look. Sports required the

The quickening pace of life and the new radical attitudes of the time although beginning to be reflected in women's clothes were not so much in men's. Most men still conformed to the style of the English gentleman.

Hats and fairly elaborate clothes were even worn by children for playing on the beach.

Children's clothes were nearly as elaborate as adults, girls wore long stockings and frilly fussy-looking dresses and hats.

The author's Father and late Aunt, both wearing long stockings and lace-up boots.

School boys clothes followed the formality of the age with high round collars, thick suits with waistcoats and watch chains, long woollen socks and lace-up shoes.

correct clothes, and men would not have dreamt of travelling without the right hats, shirts, shoes and boots. As well as the sports clothes, suits and evening dress were needed, so men as well as women took a considerable amount of luggage even for two or three days in the country, very different from the all-purpose jeans to be worn by successive generations.

Until the 19th century, men's clothes were often as flamboyant and highly decorated as women's and in some periods more so. During the Victorian age, men's clothes became more sober and less affected by drastic fashion changes. The clear division between male and female fashion established itself. Changes in men's styles were confined to the variations in the cut of jackets and trousers, the height of shirt collars or the shape of hats. The one area left for men to indulge in wearing extrovert clothes with obvious sex-appeal was the military uniforms with their bright red or dramatically dark green or blue tightly-fitting tunics, heavily trimmed with buttons and gold or silver braid. Light-coloured uniform trousers were also very tight, far tighter than the civilian ones and were worn over or tucked into high boots. By the 1900s these rather operatic looking uniforms were worn mainly for special occasions. The Boer War, which was still progressing at the beginning of the decade, had brought in the wearing of easier fitting, more practical khaki uniforms suitable for the changing style of warfare but taking away from men the impact of dashing uniforms that had been admired for so many generations.

The 1900s was the last decade of opulent living and entertaining on a grand scale that had been established over the past few centuries. Fashionable clothes were clearly for the lives of the upper classes. A large part of the population wore whatever clothes they could get. Obviously poor people shabbily dressed and even some children without shoes was a familiar and accepted sight. The idea of the masses following fashion had not begun. The various levels of the middle classes copied the upper-class style in a modified form and still adhered to the Victorian ideas of respectability in dress. Best clothes were worn on Sunday and shown off in church when new hats would be noticed. Lazing around in casual clothes on Sunday had not started and would certainly not have been approved of. Girls of seventeen and eighteen put their hair up, piling it on top of the head in the established fashion of the time.

The prosperous classes enjoyed large meals. Menus with their many courses seem excessive by modern standards and obviously gave no thought to high fat intake or cholesterol problems. Young men were sports minded and aimed at an athletic build. Chest expansion and muscle development was becoming popular, but by early middle-age many people were very overweight. Women and even some men of the period managed to conceal some of their loss of shape with corsets, pushing up or down as much of the surplus flesh as possible. Many men, however, showed large stomachs, or as they were often called, 'corporations', and further emphasised them by draping heavy watch chains from one waistcoat pocket to the other.

Children wore clothes that were nearly as elaborate as those of their elders. Girls wore lots of undergarments, long stockings and frilly fussy-looking dresses and hats. Thick suits with waistcoats, shirts with high round collars, ties and hats or caps and lace-up shoes or boots

Revolutionary ideas in fashion were introduced during the first decade but many women were not ready for the new styles. The elegantly dressed lady in 1909 shows how the established approach to fashion had only changed slightly.

The theatre and the lively music halls were still the leading forms of entertainment, the looks and shapely figures of the leading show girls were greatly admired by Edwardian men.

'Merry Widow' hat, worn by the same actress (left).

A typical Edwardian family group.

A middle-class family, all wearing the well-established styles of dress in the early years of the century, sailor suits were a very popular style for small boys.

were worn by the boys. Even for summer holidays on the beach an amazing number of elaborate clothes were worn by children and adults. Swimsuits for both sexes were very modest and covered up. Girls wore an outfit with a headscarf or cap, a long or three-quarter sleeve top, knee-length pants and long stockings.

Apart from a few upper-class women and stage personalities, only the most subtle and discreet touches of face make-up were used. An obviously made-up face was often considered one of the signs of a prostitute. Natural complexions were admired – the idea of suntanning faces and bodies would have been abhorrent. The pale skins of some of the beautiful women were greatly praised. In the summer parasols were used to keep the sun off the face.

The cinema was still in its early stages during the first ten years of the century and although it was of growing interest to the general public, the theatre and the lively music halls were still the leading forms of entertainment. When the Russian Ballet was staged in

Paris in 1909 it had a tremendous and stimulating impact. The combination of brilliant dancing and exciting colourful sets and costumes caught the mood of the time and it was to have an influence on both interior decorators and jewellery and dress designers. The looks and figures of the leading women stage personalities were greatly admired. Camille Clifford's ample curvacious figure typified the pin-up girl of the time. London's famous showgirls, the 'Gaiety Girls', were well known for their good looks and shapely curves. Many of them were paid great attention to by upper-class men and some married into aristocratic families. Men loved the showgirls with their daring low-necked costumes and fairly generous glimpses of leg. The popular songs they sang were considered rather naughty with their suggestive words. The sex appeal of the girls might seem rather tame compared with earlier and later periods but it was exciting to the men of the time who had been brought up with strict Victorian standards of modesty in behaviour and dress.

Although the first decade of the century saw the beginning of many new and revolutionary ideas in fashion, many women did not wear the new styles. They were aware of changing attitudes and the quickening pace of life but were not ready to adopt a radical new approach in their clothes. They had long-established basic ideas on dress and as yet their lives had not been affected enough to force a change in their ideas. They did not wear the extremes of the S shape at the beginning of the decade or the high waists and hobble skirts at the end. The established approach to fashion changed only slightly throughout the decade. Women taking part in active sports began to wear slightly more functional, less corseted clothes, with skirts that cleared the ground and were flared or pleated to allow for greater ease of movement.

Special outfits were introduced for motoring. Most cars were open and many country roads were still dusty or muddy. Skirts and loose topcoats were sometimes made in leather; hats were plainish, reasonably small and either had thick face veils or were worn with goggles.

Comparing photographs of everyday dress in 1900 and 1909 there are no dramatic changes. Amongst the more prosperous classes only the very fashion conscious wore the new easier fitting lines.

The dramatic changes that were to affect dress arrived in the following turbulent decade.

The 1910s

The first four and a half years of the 1910s were extremely fashion conscious and crammed in a great many changes. The new concepts of dress that had been arriving during the late 1900s, particularly Poiret's, began to take on and were developed further.

Although the mature woman with her formal social life was still well catered for – she continued to wear long straightish lines with high necks and large ornate hats – the newer styles suited a younger figure and the changing type of life they were leading. The difference between the generations was increasingly becoming more marked. Young people revelled in the faster pace of life – cars had become much more popular with women drivers as well as men, active sports were greatly enjoyed by both sexes, and there were many new dance crazes. The younger generation was very energetic and seemed determined to fill their lives as much as possible, and for this they needed easier fitting clothes. Within a couple of years new lines were being worn by fashionable younger women, hair styles became less padded and lost the Pompadour effect – they waved softly back into coiled knots rather like early classical styles. Hair was still usually long and fell at least to the shoulders when let down, sometimes much longer. Girls often claimed to be able to sit on their flowing locks. A few very advanced women cut their hair short and straight, chopped off into the 'Dutch bob', or wavy and feathery looking in the 'Titus cut', another style influenced by the classical period. Men, however, were very anti short hair, they loved long flowing tresses and it was considered a very important part of women's sex appeal.

Very wide-brimmed hats continued to be fashionable for the first few years. Many of the hat styles in 1911 were as wide and lavishly trimmed as ever, but newer looking styles in 1912 and 1913 sat deeper on the head with high crowns and smaller brims. Turban shapes and toques were very fashionable, heavily trimmed with feathers, ribbons, fruit or flowers. In the winter, deep drum shapes made in fur and rather Russian looking were popular, sometimes worn with matching fur muffs.

The new style dresses had simple round or V necks. Breasts were less emphasised and waists were much easier fitting, either in the natural place or slightly above. Legs were now the focal point and showed under narrow skirts. Very narrow skirts were called 'hobble skirts' and were a subject of endless discussion and publicity. *Punch* had drawings showing women hopping like rabbits to catch trains or buses. However, ways were soon introduced to make movement easier while still keeping the narrow look. Skirts were slit at the sides or in the front or buttoned down the front or one side with the lower buttons left open. The peg top skirt became very fashionable; it was full at the top with draped folds round the hips, it wrapped over and narrowed down the legs and was quite difficult to wear but could look very stylish on women with slim hips and long legs. The tunic line was also popular – the top flounced or flared out over the hips, sometimes with two or three flounces like large frills. The most extreme styles were wired out like a lampshade and were called 'lampshade' tunics. The tops reached to about mid-thigh and were worn over tight slit or draped skirts, either in a contrasting fabric or colour, or both. Some narrow skirts for dressy occasions or evening wear had narrow trains trailing out on the floor called 'fishtails'. Many women found these styles too extreme. It was a high fashion look and was very modified for more general wear so that afternoon and evening dresses had slightly draped effects. Tunic styles were moderately full over narrower skirts.

Between 1912 and 1914 younger women's fashions changed quite fundamentally and the

In this 1911 wedding group the bride and bridesmaid are wearing slightly younger fashions, the older women are as elaborately dressed as ever.

changes in line were further emphasised by the growing use of flimsy materials, particularly for summer dresses and evening outfits. The older generation spoke out strongly against the new fashions. Members of the medical profession drew attention to the dangers of dresses with low necklines, warning that colds, throat complaints and more serious bronchial conditions would be bound to increase alarmingly. Condemnations of the new styles were also made from pulpits and the Pope expressed his disapproval of scanty dresses with low necklines. Far from modifying the new directions in fashion, they became even more daring. Some were fantasy clothes and worn only by the ultra fashion-conscious, such as baggy harem trousers with brocade or embroidered lampshade tunics, widely sashed at the waist and worn with draped turbans and jewelled slippers, making the wearer look like a figure from the Arabian Nights. These outfits made good publicity pictures but were rarely worn.

Dancing was very popular and had a strong influence on fashion. The tremendous appeal of the Russian ballet was at its height and Russian-style tunics in vivid coloured embroidered silk, or heavy brocade lavishly trimmed with fur were worn by many fashionable women. The tango was thought very dramatic and considered erotic and quite sinful by some people. It helped popularise vampish-looking evening dresses, heavily trimmed with beads and fringe and worn with Spanish-style jewelled combs in the hair or headbands sprouting groups of feathers. The Castles, the famous American dancing couple, helped to spread many of the new dance crazes with their skilful demonstrations. Magazines showed a series of photographs of the couple going through the steps of the dances stage by stage to help people who wanted to practise at home. Irene Castle was good-looking and suited many of the latest fashions. She

The straighter simpler lines of the late 1900s carried on into the early 1910s. The sketch from *La Mode Illustrée* for September 1910 shows how hair styles had become less padded and lost the Pompadour effect.

Many of the hat styles of 1911 still had very wide brims and lavish trimmings.

was one of the first well-known women to bob her hair and many women copied her style of dressing as well as her dancing skills. Ragtime music, the forerunner of jazz, started in America in the 1900s and swept Europe in the early 1910s. Ragtime was the basis of many of the new dance crazes, the animal dances imitating some form of animal movement, the 'Grizzly Bear', the 'Bunny Hug' and the 'Turkey Trot'. These energetic dances needed easy fitting dresses with long slits to enable women to do the movements. Calves and flashes of knees were now seen on dance floors. It was all too much for many of the older generation. Scanty clothes, animal dances, raucous Ragtime music and the flippant attitude of some of the young – grave doubts about the future were expressed with fears as to where society was heading. The direction it was going in was rather ironically given in the words of one of the popular songs, 'Alexander's Ragtime Band':

Come on and hear, come on and hear
Alexander's Ragtime Band.
Come on and hear, come on and hear,
It's the best band in the land.

You can hear a bugle call like you never heard before,
Hear a bugle call that will make you want to go to war.

By 1914 the fashion changes of the early 1910s had affected the clothes most women wore

New hat shapes in 1912 and 1913 sat deeper on the head with higher crowns and deeper brims.

Ways were introduced to make movement easier in the narrow skirts while still keeping the narrow look. Draped and wrapped-over peg top skirts became very fashionable.

12ᵉ Année. N° 276.
(Le 1ᵉʳ et le 15 de chaque mois.)

15 Juillet 1912.
(Le 1ᵉʳ et le 15 de chaque mois.)

ROBES D'ÉTÉ
VUES AUX COURSES

En crêpe de chine noir.
Revers, parements blancs.

En crêpe de chine blanc.
Revers, parements noirs.

This *Femina* cover featured two very elegant variations of tunic line. These styles with their moderately full tops and slightly draped skirts showed how a high fashion line was modified into a more wearable form.

and established ways of dressing were brought up-to-date by adapting them to the new silhouette. Most hairstyles were simpler and less padded. Hats were plainer and smaller. Figures were still corseted but they were straighter, flatter corsets designed to narrow the hips rather than shape the bust and waist. Blouse and dress bodices were easier fitting and less decorated; the high boned collars were replaced by lower necklines but deep V-necks were still considered too daring by many women. Tailored suits were firmly established clothes for most women; jackets became less tightly figure shaped and narrow skirts were wrapped over or slit to allow for comfortable walking. Most prosperous women still had their clothes individually made by dressmakers and tailors but department stores selling ready-made clothes began to attract a growing clientele in England and America. Accessories such as gloves, handbags and furs, although still formal and rich looking, were less opulent than those worn during the 1900s.

Class distinction through dress was clearly marked but it was not quite so blatant as it had been at the beginning of the century. The pace of everyday life, particularly in the cities, had speeded up. Women were far more active and couldn't lead their busier lives in the fashions of the early 1900s.

The clothes women wore for active sports were still restricting by later standards but they were becoming a little easier; the less corseted lines and the slightly shorter skirts gave women more freedom of movement than the rigid lines of the previous decade; even swimming costumes were a little less covered up.

The fashions for summer 1914 were very soft and feminine. Looking back, perhaps nostalgically after the horrors of the war, some men thought women had never looked so lovely. Hair styles had side curls on to the face known as 'kiss curls'. Toque-shaped hats were

Dance crazes had an influence on fashion. The Castles, the famous American dancing couple demonstrated many of the new dance steps, and Irene Castle's fashions were copied by many.

often trimmed with flowers. Many blouses and dresses had lingerie looking trimmings of frills or broderie anglaise. The silhouette was softening, tunic styles and draped peg top skirts were still fashionable but they were easier looking and less contrived. Very girlish dresses with wider, fuller skirts, short enough to show the ankles, were beginning to be worn. Elaine Williams, a Canadian lady visiting London as a young girl that summer, remembers how she and her friends still tried to get on buses without showing their ankles. Ankles were no longer such a novelty in London. A Cockney bus conductor shouted out cheekily, 'Step along, ladies; ankles ain't no treat to me'. Far more leg was soon to be shown by the bus conductresses or 'clippies' who were to take over from the men during the war years.

The beginning of the First World War had no immediate impact on fashion apart from civilians in the battle areas. The population was not affected as it was to be in later wars. Food rationing and bombing did not begin until the second half of the war and America did not become involved until 1917. Clothes had already become easier fitting by the time the war started; only the long narrow skirts were too restricting to women about to lead a much more active life. By 1915 shorter, full skirts between low calf and ankle length were being worn by many women. During the next couple of years they became slightly shorter, although many older women continued to wear ankle length and dresses that were a modified version of the Edwardian styles. Easy fitting, full-skirted dresses, tailored suits and less elaborate hats and blouses became the basic more practical styles of the time. With the shorter skirts buttoned or laced calf-high boots showed. They were made in leather and had cloth gaitered effects, buttoning up the calf, usually in grey, beige or cream, known as cloth top boots. Stockings also showed and were in dark-coloured cotton or wool in the winter, light-coloured cotton, particularly white, in the summer. Sheer silk stockings were worn by the better-off

Clothes worn for active sports were still restricting but they were becoming a little easier. Knitted cardigans and shorter skirts gave women more freedom of movement.

fashionable women. Shoes laced up the front or had several straps fastening across. Dressier shoe styles had fancy bows, rosettes or buckles in the front and some cross-laced up the leg like ballet shoes. Louis heels were still popular but higher, straighter heels were also being worn. Hat fashions continued throughout the war years and although considered quite simple at the time, were elaborate and fussy by later standards. The deep crowns and narrow brims continued but with the full skirted silhouette, wider brimmed styles came back into fashion but they were not as big or heavily trimmed as the styles worn at the beginning of the decade. The new designs were made in felt or straw and trimmed with ribbons. The brims were often turned up at the back, and the front of the hat was tilted forward or to one side. They were sometimes called 'shepherdess' hats, looking rather like the hats worn by shepherdesses in romantic 19th-century paintings. Large squashy looking berets became very popular. They were easy to wear, warm and practical, youthful looking and suited the plainer clothes many women were wearing.

As the war continued, more women joined the armed forces, trained as nurses or undertook some kind of war work. Women driving military vehicles and ambulances, nurses rushing to and from duty, and the crowds of women in overalls busily producing shells, bombs and tanks in the armament factories, known as 'working on munitions', all soon became accepted everyday sights in their functional clothes. The old, long-established idea of class distinction in dress became somewhat confused. Women of all classes now wore the same clothes when on duty in the Services or working in the factories. Their off-duty clothes and the clothes worn by many women not directly involved in war work tended to be simpler. It was often considered unpatriotic to spend too much time and money on clothes. The continual reminder of the ever-growing death toll with the published lists in the papers, may have made many women feel that too much attention to fashion was flippant and very inappropriate in

The tunic line in its most extreme form – 'lampshade' top over tight trailing 'fishtail' skirt.

the sombre atmosphere of the time. Wearing opulent-looking clothes was now often thought *nouveau riche*. Remarks were made about the wives of war profiteers dressing too grandly. There was a new kind of inverted snobbery which did not approve of displaying wealth and rank in dress, very different from the Edwardian period. Quite a lot of girls from modest backgrounds were earning comparatively high wages in the munition factories and quite naturally spent some of their money on clothes. Fur coats, particularly musquash, were very popular with some of these girls and remarks were made about them trying to ape their betters.

The fashions for summer 1914 were very feminine, the silhouette was softening, hats were trimmed with flowers, lingerie looking frills and broderie anglais were used on dresses and blouses.

Soft and pretty clothes were considered right to cheer up the men on leave. Magazines such as the *Sketch* and the *Bystander* showed drawings of pretty women in girlish-looking dresses with admiring looks on their faces surrounding a man in uniform, or a coy-looking girl on her own with a handsome officer about to approach her. Military terms were used as captions under these drawings. The girls surrounding the man in uniform were captioned 'An Enveloping Movement' and the officer waiting to stop the coy girl was called 'The Christmas Sniper'.

Despite anti-fashion attitudes and the many changes in life during the war, fashion changes did continue and new designers began to make a name for themselves. Chanel had been noticed in some French social circles even before she became known as a designer. Her own individual style of dress was very advanced for the time. Like Poiret she believed in uncorseted, easy fitting clothes but unlike Poiret who loved exotic influences, Chanel liked deliberate understatement. Her own clothes had a distinct style. She wore simple, belted raincoats and soft pull-on hats or berets, open-necked plain shirts like men's sports shirts, and simple-looking English blazers or cardigans in quiet colours such as beige, grey and navy. Other fashion-conscious women of the time were still wearing quite elaborate outfits and ornate hats. Far from looking out of place, Chanel managed to make many women feel overdressed. She also looked very young and appealing in a boyish kind of way. She had already started many of the basic ideas on dress that she was going to popularise all over the world. Variations on these ideas are still being used in fashion over 60 years later. Chanel's early selling was done from a small shop in Deauville where she sold hats and later simple outfits. Early in the war, women who evacuated to Deauville started buying her clothes with their easy relaxed looking lines. Later Chanel moved to Paris and her designs were soon appearing in the leading fashion magazines. By 1916 her simple tops, skirts and chemise dresses were becoming known internationally. The chemise dress was to be a basic line of the future. It was simple, if not more simple than many of the undergarments of a few years earlier with a round or straight across boat-shaped neck, it hung loose and easy fitting with a belt or fabric tie lightly marking a high, natural or lowish waist. The skirt was moderately full and mid to lower calf length. A little embroidery was used on some styles or fabric inserts in contrasting materials or colours. Material loops and fabric covered buttons were sometimes used as fastenings or for decoration. The styles may seem rather fussy by later standards but were very simple and youthful looking at the time.

With the establishment of much simpler clothes home dressmaking became more popular. Loose fitting chemise dresses and blouses were the easiest clothes to make. Blouses were as popular as ever and very feminine looking, but unlike the styles of the 1900s with their high necks, long sleeves and clearly corseted figures, the blouses of the mid 1910s had a soft, loose almost lingerie look. Fabrics, such as voile, crepe and silk crêpe-de-Chine, were used for styles with round, deep V or crossover necklines. When collars were used they were delicate looking, simple round shapes or flimsy sailor collars with matching or contrasting ties fastening into low floppy bows. Many summer styles had loose short sleeves. Lace was popular as a trimming on collars and cuffs. A few rows of tucks or pleats and a little embroidery were sometimes used on the fronts of some styles.

Knitted cardigans and pullovers had been worn before the war, mainly for sportswear such as golf and tennis. During the war, knitted scarves, socks and pullovers were produced in

Young fashions for autumn 1913 were noticeably more easy fitting with skirts shortened to show feet and ankles.

" Bright and breezy "

The cheerful group on the postcard shows how class distinction through dress was not quite as blatant as it had been at the beginning of the century.

great quantities by home knitters for the armed forces. Women also started knitting tops and cardigans for themselves and found them extremely useful, particularly when fuel became scarce. Knitted tops became a firmly established part of many women's wardrobes and they were used as fashion items. Knitted jumpers with boat-shaped necklines, fairly loose fitting in plain knitting, stripes, pattern effects or trimmed with contrasting fabrics such as fur or fringe and teamed with a simple skirt and a pull-on hat or beret, became a popular modern looking style of dressing.

During the last two years of the war a new alternative silhouette was introduced by the Paris designers. It was a barrel-shaped line. The bodice was easy fitting with a lightly marked slightly high waist; the line curved out from the waist over the hips and narrowed to a calf length hemline. The idea of women wanting to give themselves a barrel-shaped silhouette would have been almost incomprehensible to the devotees of the S-shape only a decade before. It was not an easy line to wear and had a very limited success in its more extreme form but the idea of an easy fitting line narrowing to the hem rather than flaring out remained as a fashion influence for a few years.

By 1918 women's clothes had become simpler and more functional than anything the suffragettes at the beginning of the decade could have imagined. Any idea of holding back on women's emancipation had been outdated by their involvement in the war effort. Women in England were given the vote at last, although for the first few years it was only given to married women over 30 who were house owners.

Women's emancipation was also reflected in the growing popularity of cutting hair short. Bobbing hair was still extremely controversial in America and Europe; some women were simply forbidden to have theirs bobbed. The challenge was often too much, it was cut, and rows with disapproving fathers and husbands followed. All to no avail – bobbed heads continued to multiply.

As the war progressed more women joined the armed forces, and women of all classes were identically dressed.

The appearance of women war workers in overalls, busily producing shells, bombs and tanks in the armament factories, soon became an accepted everyday sight.

The simple chemise dress was the new basic line. It hung loose with the waistline only lightly marked. Girls' clothing also followed the new line – their head-fitting hats and bobbed hair was very advanced.

Large squashy berets were a practical and youthful-
looking war-time style. The one illustrated was worn
by Pearl White, the heroine whose adventures were
regularly followed by the early cinema audiences.

Bobbed hair was still a controversial fashion. Many
women arranged the front and side of the hair in the
bobbed style but kept the back long and pulled
into a roll.

A very different-looking fashionable woman had emerged by the end of the war. A man
going off to war in the summer of 1914, leaving his girlfriend in her soft frilly dress with its
long draped skirt and rose trimmed toque might have been staggered to be greeted by one of
the new modern young women with bobbed hair, fairly obvious face make-up, straightish calf
length, chemise dress and possibly smoking a cigarette through a long holder.

Make-up was gradually becoming more acceptable. In John Galsworthy's *On Forsyte
Change* Soames notes disapprovingly that towards the end of the war women with face make-
up were becoming more common and how it had been one of the signs of a loose woman in
his young days. Early in 1919 English *Vogue* comments on the amount of make-up worn by
some French women and also on their very short skirts. The length was still well below the
knee but must have been noticeably shorter than was generally worn in England. In Colette's
Cheri the scanty clothes, make-up and night club life at the end of the war are also
commented on unfavourably compared to the grander style of life at the beginning of the
century. It was thought to be tawdry and the attitude of the young cynical and disillusioned.
The World War changed the social pattern more completely than at any time since the
French Revolution. Fashion had changed more in a few years than is usual over several
decades.

Children's fashions followed the fundamental change towards simpler easier-fitting clothes. Girls' dresses still had quite elaborate design details such as fancy collars, cuffs and lace and ribbon trimmings but the basic cut became quite loose and easy with no waist or with sashes or belts lightly marking the hip line. The length finished just above the knee and the overall look was very similar to that which women were going to wear in the following decade. During the 1910s there was far more scope for teenage dressing, the general fashion lines being much more suitable than the Edwardian styles had been with their curved corseted lines. Dresses and blouses with their soft fullish bodices and flared, calf-length skirts looked equally good on a girl of seventeen or a woman of thirty. Girls in their teens still usually had long hair which was taken back and tied with a bow at the nape of the neck; the controlled hair was then allowed to fall down the back in a group of curls or a plait. When girls walked about the hair flapped up and down. Teenage girls were often called 'flappers', and later all kinds of modern looking young women became known as this.

Boys' clothes also became less restricting and covered up, particularly for casual and holiday wear. They benefited from the home knitting and wore pullovers, scarves and socks for many more occasions instead of the formal buttoned-up suits and waistcoats with stiff collared shirts of the earlier 1900s. Teenage boys had little opportunity to wear special fashions – many boys were in uniform by the time they were in their late teens.

There were no great changes in men's fashions in the early 1910s. The gentlemanly conformist style of dressing became even more established. Slightly dandified variations such as braided suits, capes and hats, so popular at the turn of the century, were greatly modified. The height of good dressing became the exact degree of correctness in dress, the cut and quality of the fabric in suits and coats, perfectly shaped hats in the best felts, the finest leathers and workmanship in bespoke shoes and boots. Shirts and ties were chosen with great care to match or tone perfectly. Gloves in soft leather and the right toning colour were always worn or carried. English under-statement with its perfection in cut and quality was the pinnacle of stylishness for men. Inferior quality fabrics or loudness in the colour of shoes, socks or shirts or check suitings that were too strongly defined, were all give-away signs in men's dress and the wearers often condemned for being sadly lacking in taste. The English were particularly superior about the right clothes and confident that their style was unquestionably the best.

Although the top quality of the best British men's clothes could not be afforded by many of the middle classes, the style of dress and the attitudes of correctness was copied. During the late 1910s my father started work in an insurance office. Heads of departments came to work in black jackets, black striped trousers and stiff-looking shirts with high standing collar bands which turned over in the front like envelope points but stuck out, and were known as wing collars; ordinary clerks all wore stiff, round, white collars. The departments worked on Saturday mornings when very slightly less formal looking clothes could be worn. One friend of my father unwisely wore a striped shirt, a very moderate stripe but at the time a fairly definite break with conformity. He was told in no uncertain terms by the head of the department that he was in a business house not a music-hall and never to wear such a shirt to work again and to keep out of sight for the rest of the morning. Dickensian attitudes like these persisted well into the early decades of the century.

Apart from special parades, formal functions and ceremonial occasions, dashing ornate

G.BARBIER 1913

This bathing dress of 1913 would have been considered daringly revealing at the time.

Officers often wore wide topped riding breeches,
ankle boots and high fastening leather gaiters.

All the details of an officer's kit was clearly laid down,
and Burberry's in London produced special raincoats.

uniforms were a thing of the past by the time the First World War started. Most countries
had adopted some shade of khaki or grey. The German army wore what was called field grey.
In August 1914 as they advanced against Belgium they were often described as 'the advancing
hordes of field grey'. In the atmosphere of drummed up patriotic feeling, many men rushed
to join the armed forces and felt quite gallant in their uniforms. Public schools in England
had military cadet forces, the OTC – Officers Training Corps. Senior boys of eighteen,
anxious to join up, went into the Services as officers or very quickly became one. Khaki shirts
and ties were worn and tunic jackets were sometimes tailored individually to give a perfect fit.
Wide polished leather belts were worn round the waist, known as 'Sam Browns', matching
leather straps went across the chest and back and there was a leather revolver holster at the
back just below the belt. Officers' caps were deliberately pulled down and slightly squashed at
the sides by some young men who felt it gave a more debonair look. With the tunic jackets,
matching trousers or wide topped riding breeches were worn. Over the narrow legs of the
breeches, bands of khaki material were bound round up to the knees and these were known
as 'puttees'. Leather ankle boots were worn with puttees. Many officers preferred leather
gaiters fastening up the leg, or knee-high leather boots with the fronts laced from the middle

The differences in the uniforms worn by ordinary soldiers and officers were far less than in earlier periods, but non-commissioned ranks always wore 'puttees', bands of khaki material bound round the legs.

As the war dragged on the ever-growing death toll and the thousands of men injured finished many men's early admiration for military styles of dress.

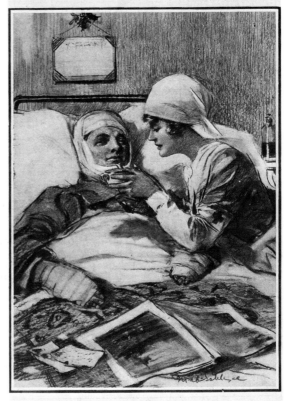

His Christmas Dinner, 1917

—AND <u>HE</u> THINKS HIMSELF LUCKY!

of the foot, called 'field boots'. Other officers wore pull-on long boots like classic riding or polo boots. Quite a few men spent several years wearing riding breeches and boots but had never ridden a horse in their lives. Scott Fitzgerald in one of his stories about an American girl during the war who was paid great attention to by young officers, noted with amusement that some young Air Force pilots, eager to impress and look dashing, wore spurs on their long boots. The spurs could hardly have been needed as an aid to flying planes.

All the details of officers' kit were clearly laid down. Certain required items were specially produced by well-known firms. A good raincoat was essential. Burberry's in London produced such a coat, the famous trench coat. Men continued to wear their trench coats after the war and women also started wearing them. Apart from slight variations in cut and length to fit into fashion changes, the basic style has remained the same and is still a bestseller today and is known, admired and copied all over the world. The uniforms of ordinary soldiers were not as good quality or as stylish as the officers', but the differences were far less than in earlier periods. The basic khaki caps, tunics and trousers were similar and the cloth puttees were wound round the trouser legs to calf length. Great care had to be taken to do this well, particularly for parades. It was an acquired knack.

Men's hair was short before the war started but even shorter hair was insisted on in the armed forces. Ordinary soldiers were given an extreme version of the short back and sides cut and were shorn right up the back and the sides of the head with clippers. Neat moustaches were allowed and were quite popular with all ranks. They helped make very young faced sergeants and officers look slightly more mature. By the end of the war, men were sick of uniforms. All the early appeal of wearing gallant uniforms and going off to a war that was supposed to be over by the first Christmas had gone. The horrors of war quickly finished any admiration for military styles of dress, and the clothes that were popular in the post-war period were as remote from this as possible.

Commercial entertainment grew and developed during the 1910s. Music-halls were still very popular but rather more sophisticated musical shows with spectacular sets and costumes captured the public imagination and cheered up wartime audiences. The female stars were often popular in society circles and their looks and clothes publicised and copied. The cinema was also expanding and developing rapidly. Film stars were becoming well known by all classes. The adventures of Pearl White, the good girl heroine, were followed regularly by the

Business men worked in very formal looking suits and white shirts with high standing collars.

Men's fashions in the 1910s followed the gentlemanly conformist style.

Theda Barr was one of the early 'vamps', the wicked looking ladies of the early cinema with heavily outlined eyes and daring dresses.

Mary Pickford with her girlish sweet looks was dubbed the world's sweetheart. Many girls attempted to copy her looks and fashions and her famous hairstyle.

fast-growing cinema audiences. Vamps, the rather wicked sultry looking ladies with heavily outlined eyes, draped headbands and wearing dark exotic dresses and smoking through long cigarette holders, were often thought to be the height of worldly sophistication. Mary Pickford, with her girlish sweet looks and tumbling shoulder-length blonde curls, was dubbed the world's sweetheart. Many teenage girls tried hard to look like Mary Pickford, copying her type of dresses and the famous hairstyle. The cinema was beginning to be an important influence on women's looks and fashions.

America, although not rivalling Europe as a centre for creative fashion, was pushing ahead in the general developments in clothes and looks. America's growing population was less hidebound by class divisions. Hard work and drive were creating prosperity at a mass level, and the fashion industry was beginning to cater for this growing market. Ready-to-wear clothes had always been considered poor; they were often in low quality fabrics, very basic in cut and lacking in good design. This began to change. American ready-made clothes started to offer cheap dresses, suits and coats with quite good styling and cut, long before Europe became involved in mass-produced clothes. The new industry grew quickly. It was a boon to American women; many more could now afford to follow fashion and change their styles from season to season. It was the beginning of important changes in attitude towards following fashion, and a lessening of the authority and exclusiveness of the couture houses and top tailors and dressmakers.

America was also advanced in the growing popularity of hairdressers and the use of cosmetics and beauty parlours were opening up. More obviously waved and dyed hair was becoming acceptable. Women were learning how to use make-up and be able to copy the looks of their favourite film stars. Many Americans still held strong puritanical views and did not approve of dyed hair and face make-up. There were many differences of opinion and clashes of will in families on these subjects.

A.E.MARTY

There was no one predominant line for 1919 evening dresses. Shapes varied from the very full to the very narrow and skirt lengths ranged from the middle of the calf to the ankles.

Fashions in 1919 were rather confused and lacking in direction. The easy fitting, simple chemise dress, varying in skirt fullness and length, was well established and would be developed further, but there were attempts to revive styles from earlier in the decade and take up where fashion had left off in 1914. Peg-top hip drapery was revived but the line did not suit the calf-length hem, the proportions looked wrong and tended to make women look unnecessarily hippy. The tunic line was also used in suit jackets that curved out over the hips like a flared riding jacket. Bodices, however, were flatter than before the war and the waist less shaped. Again, the basic easy fit did not suit the hip emphasis. Designers differed widely from one another, some showing shorter, straighter lines, others long draped styles; very full skirts were promoted by some fashion houses, others showed skirts almost as long and tight as the hobble skirts. The vagaries and contradictions in the early post-war fashions, may have been a reflection of the times with their financial and political instability, or merely that after the sombre war years women wanted to catch up and enjoy the feeling of plenty in fashion and to be shown a great variety before settling down to more orderly fashion changes. For everyday wear, however, most women continued to wear easy familiar styles. Tailored suits were established basic items. Toque and beret style hats continued to be popular, often fussily trimmed with feather, flowers and veils. Three-cornered shaped hats, similar to those worn by men in the 18th century became fashionable; the angular lines were sometimes softened with veiling. Quite large hats were worn during the first post-war summer with its revived social

By 1919 women's clothes had become simpler and more functional than ever could have been envisaged at the beginning of the decade.

occasions. They were very girlish looking with soft wavy brims often trimmed or completely made with lace. Some women's heads, slightly tilted, looked coyly through the lace brims of their hats.

Evening dress was the area where prosperous fashion-conscious women felt they could indulge in several new outfits and try some of the wide variety of new styles. In the early postwar atmosphere of liberation there were many opportunities to wear evening dresses at receptions, private parties and dances. Dancing was more popular than ever. Ragtime was developing into jazz, young people flocked to dance to the new blaring jazz bands, dance halls opened all over America and Europe and the more sophisticated night life in the clubs became established in major cities.

There was no predominant line for evening dresses; most styles were bare topped and often sleeveless with straight across necklines or held up with straps, but the rest of the dress lines differed widely. Shapes ranged from very full flouncy skirts to straight beaded chemises. More complicated designs had transparent over-skirts or draped and folded peg-top skirts. Lengths varied from mid-calf to ankle length or had uneven hemlines. Some dresses with quite short skirts had narrow loose back panels trailing onto the floor. These were quite hazardous on the dance floor; other dresses had side panels falling in waterfall folds which finished above, below or at the same length as the skirt hem. Women added a surprising amount of decorative accessories to their rather fussy-looking dresses. Headbands were very popular either made in the same material as the dress or a suitable contrasting fabric such as satin or velvet; some headbands were embroidered with beads and trimmed with a feather or a group of feathers. The bands were worn straight across the forehead and the sides of the hairstyles, whether bobbed or not, were waved onto the cheeks. Embroidered or fringed handbags hung from the wrists and quite a lot of jewellery was worn including dangling earrings, long necklaces and bracelets. A large ostrich feather was sometimes carried and used as a fan. Evening cloaks, in fabrics such as velvet, satin or brocade, were often worn to complete outfits. They usually wrapped over and were held close, giving a cocoon shape. They were often trimmed with fur, particularly fox. Large fox collars were very popular, and some evening wraps also had fox cuffs and edgings round the front and hem creating quite a sumptuous look. There was much posing and arranging and rearranging of wraps. They were sometimes draped low to show one or both shoulders, one hand holding it closed, the other holding a long cigarette holder.

Major fashion changes had taken place by the end of the second decade of the century. Social and political developments together with the First World War had forced a simpler more practical style of dressing onto women of all ages and classes. Easy fitting garments, showing necks, arms and legs, were established as basic necessities in clothes and although attempts had been made to re-introduce more elaborate fashions, clothes had stayed practical enough for women to lead active lives. A degree of uniformity and even drabness had been accepted as part of the more practical way of dressing. By 1920 the character of the 20th century had emerged and clothes had adapted to fit in with it.

The 1920s

This *Punch* drawing in February 1920 sets the tone of
the decade – the scanty look of the woman's dress,
and the couples' determination to enjoy themselves.

The Roaring Twenties are usually thought of as a good-time period, the jazz age of dancing, wild parties and looser morals, peopled by the bright post-war generation often known as 'the bright young things'. This world, immortalised in books and plays, was confined mainly to the middle and upper classes. The social changes that had been accelerated by the war spread more slowly amongst the rest of the population and were not as far reaching as changes that followed the Second World War.

For a lot of people the 1920s were far from fun. Some men returned from the war disabled mentally or physically by their experiences. There were many widows and women whose potential husbands had been killed in the war. The short-lived post-war boom in industry was quickly followed by the slump with growing unemployment. Life was hard for many, and there was little money available for clothes, let alone following the latest fashions.

The 1920s have been portrayed many times in plays, films and on television. Flirty flappers in helmet-shaped cloche hats and low-waisted, knee-length dresses, breaking into the Charleston dance on the slightest pretext is a popular idea of young women throughout the decade. In fact the very short straight silhouette belongs to the second half of the twenties. During the first four or five years a wide variety of quite elaborate styles were worn by fashionable women. At the beginning of the decade many women still had long hair worn in several different styles. It was taken into a knot just below the crown and held with a fancy comb giving a slightly Spanish look that went very well with the popular fringed Spanish shawls and fringed evening dresses; or the hair was curled onto the forehead and cheeks and went softly back into a loose roll or bun. This style was easily adapted for the evening with the addition across the forehead of a decorative band or scarf. These were still very popular and were easier to attach and hold in position with long hair. Some women, eager to look modern but nervous about bobbing their hair, cut the front and side short but kept the back long, bobbing in stages. Once they and their husbands or fathers got used to the look of short hair from the front, they went on to the next stage and cut the back.

Most hats sat well down on the head but the shapes of the crowns and brims were quite varied. Toque and beret styles continued but rather theatrical looking hats were also popular. They had large brims which were turned up off the face and were trimmed with bunches of ribbons or feathers. They were called Cavalier or Musketeer hats and were thought to be dashing looking and inspired by the styles of the 17th century. More uniform hat shapes with deeper crowns had gained in popularity by 1922-23 and although still differing in brim widths and trimmings, they were clearly the forerunners of the famous helmet cloches of the later twenties.

In 1922 and 1923 designers made attempts to bring back more ornate fashions with longer skirts.

Queen Mary continued to wear the styles of the early 1910s, she never adopted the cloche hat and the shorter skirts worn by the woman in the background.

The unemphasised breasts and waists were well established in fashion by 1920 and remained so throughout the decade but hipline waists took several years to establish themselves. During the first few years many dresses and blouses and skirts had lightly indicated normal waistlines. Skirt fullness ranged from slim wrapover styles worn with long riding-shaped jackets to dresses with moderately full skirts and side drapes or loose hanging panels at one or both sides. Very full bouffant afternoon and evening dresses known as 'picture frocks' were very fashionable and considered romantic looking, and like some of the hat styles of the time they were thought to be inspired by historic costume.

Skirt lengths were always well below the knee. In 1921 *Women's Pictorial* talks about 'today's brief skirts just below the knee'. Looking at the illustrations, the shortest are mid to upper calf length. Many women were still wearing longer lengths and in 1922 attempts were made by some designers to reintroduce the pre-war ankle length.

The fashionable ideal for women in the early post-war years was young and girlish with an adolescent figure. Girls in their late teens who would once have been considered gauche and under-developed were now admired. Older women slimmed and tried to look younger. The stately mature woman with her well-rounded figure was now often thought dowdy and matronly. Mannerisms and poses also changed. Women stood with their pelvis pushed slightly forward, shoulders rather hunched and one hand resting on the hip, giving a concave look to the chest and torso. Fleur in the *Forsyte Saga* typified many of the new attitudes in women, irritating her father Soames with her modern slang, laughing at his Victorian views and calling him a 'scream'.

The new modern ideas on dress and behaviour were certainly not held by everybody. Many men and women were still very conservative in outlook and considered any form of showing off with clothes undesirable. In an interview for *Women's Pictorial*, in January 1923, Lady

Fashions in the early twenties were still quite elaborate, hair styles, hats and skirt shapes varied.

Astor expressed her views on clothes. These views seem priggish and even laughable by later standards but many of her ideas were shared by the upper classes, particularly in Britain: 'Everyone wants to be nicely dressed. It is right that they should. Nice clothes are the expression of a nice mind. When you get beyond wanting to be just nicely dressed you are getting away from the motive for pretty dresses. It isn't really at all nice to want to make anyone feel uncomfortable and that is all that happens when your object is merely to out-shine or out-do. You simply want to cause envy and jealousy. You may say you want to cause admiration; admiration for what? Your character or your clothes or your figure? It must be one of these things, but a truly fine character never thinks of being admired, only the egotist does that. To have clothes admired as clothes is sheer vulgarity. To wish to attract attention to your figure is just the desire to attract the male sex through its most vulnerable point. Is that really worth doing? Don't we women have to pay for these methods in the long run?'

Perhaps as a reaction to the brasher post-war world, designers in 1922 and 1923 made further attempts to bring back more elaborate fashions influenced by period costume. Skirts were definitely longer, ankle length or just above. Periods from ancient Greece to the 1880s were scanned for design ideas. The publicity over the excavations in Tutankhamen's tomb helped popularise ancient Egyptian influences. Egyptian style embroideries and motifs were

Evening outfit with strong Spanish influence – rose at
the waist, flimsy shawl and lace fan.

used on dresses, jackets and cloaks. Jewellery, particularly to wear with evening dresses,
copied old Egyptian designs and used them for long earrings, necklaces and snake-shaped
bracelets or fancy bangles worn singly or in groups round the wrists or round the upper arm
and called 'slave bangles'. In November 1922 *Harper's Bazaar* devoted its cover, drawn by
Erté, and many inside pages to fancy-dress looking fashions. Outfits were described as
'Medieval', 'Renaissance' or 'Victorian'. Full skirted or draped evening dresses with hip line
interest were written about as being like 'the ones Grandma wore'. It was only the skirts of
these dresses that faintly resembled Victorian styles. The bodices with their straight across
necklines, flat chests and low waists, were very much of the 1920s.

   With the costume-look designers were trying hard to promote, there was a temporary swing
away from short hair. Longer styles were more suited to the fashions but were rather severe
looking. They were parted in the middle and scraped back into a tidy knot at the back of the
neck and were only flattering to women with good features and well-shaped heads.

   The attempts to return to more elaborate clothes had a very limited success. It was against
the general development in women's emancipation and the faster pace of life. Long skirts
were associated with the older generation and the pre-war world. Fashionable younger women
had only just got used to the mid and upper calf lengths and older and more conservative

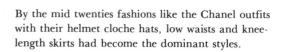

The bob was shortened into
completely bare necked styles,
sometimes cut with a neat point on
the cheeks. The girl below has the
severe Eton crop.

By the mid twenties fashions like the Chanel outfits
with their helmet cloche hats, low waists and knee-
length skirts had become the dominant styles.

women had never worn skirts shorter than lower calf which they thought practical without being too modern.

There was a general confusion over lengths for a year or two. By the autumn of 1924 they were definitely getting shorter. The most advanced styles were about two inches below the knee. The following year they reached the knees. Never in recorded history had women shown bare legs and it was to be another 40 years before the length was surpassed by the mini skirts of the sixties. Like the mini, very short skirts of the 1920s caused a sensation. In some respects they had an even greater impact. Many people had grown up with Victorian ideas of dress and skirts that trailed on the ground and had been worn as recently as the early 1910s and could be remembered even by the young generation in their twenties.

Humorous magazines were full of drawings showing the effects confident young women were causing in their short skirts. They were shown walking boldly down the streets with older women giving hostile stares, or they would be illustrated sitting on a train blatantly showing knees and thighs to the horror and indignation of elderly gentlemen whose monocles had fallen from their eyes in shock. My mother remembers wearing the daring new length on a visit to Cornwall. Her cousin gasped when they met at the railway station and was careful to stand slightly in front of her when she was introduced to her friends in case they noticed and disapproved of her very short skirt.

By 1925 the straight uncluttered silhouette with a low or no waistline had become the dominant line for day and evening clothes. Hair styles were shorter than ever. The bob had been shortened into the shingle or Eton crop. Both styles showed the ears, the shape of the skull and completely bare necks and were almost as short as the men's short back and sides cut. The shingle was slightly longer on top, usually waved and sometimes cut to allow waves or soft curls to fall onto the cheeks. The Eton crop was more severe; parted at the side, it was brushed straight back and rubbed with brilliantine to give a very sleek, ultra neat appearance which sometimes looked hard and masculine. Over the very short hair went the helmet cloche hats which came right down to the eyebrows and were shaped onto the nape of the neck, concealing all the hair except for a neat wave or point on the cheeks. During the mid and late twenties, deep cloche hats were almost universally worn. Films and plays produced in recent years and set in the 1920s rarely show cloches pulled right down, they are usually incorrectly worn further back on the head.

Obvious face make-up was becoming more acceptable although *Women's Pictorial* in 1921 mentions 'painted flappers' rather disapprovingly and in 1923 comments on the amount of make-up some women were wearing, particularly lipstick. By the mid twenties many fashionable women were using cosmetics freely and sometimes rather crudely. Faces were powdered with rouged cheeks and eyebrows were pencilled. Some women shaved off their eyebrows and pencilled an arched shape above the natural place, giving them a permanently surprised look. Eyelids were shadowed and lips were bright red and drawn into a more pointed shape known as a 'Cupid's bow' or 'rosebud'.

During the early twenties, a slight suntan began to be admired and the prosperous classes started to go to Mediterranean resorts in the summer months rather than in the winter and spring which had been the fashionable seasons before the First World War. As the twenties progressed, sunbathing became more and more popular. It was considered smart to be in the South of France or on the Venice Lido in July and August. *Vogue* and *Harper's Bazaar*

Dress bodices were flat chested but skirt designs were influenced by period costume, the woman's long skirt had a slightly medieval look.

The straight knee-length silhouette was adopted for wedding dresses but the veil attached to the head-dress still trailed on to the floor.

showed special resort clothes including trousers, shorts and sleeveless tops. Photographs of well-known women on holiday looking very suntanned and wearing the new emancipated casual clothes were shown in the late summer issues of the magazines with admiring comments in the captions on the women's suntans. With their simple brief looking clothes in light colours a dark tan was very effective and quite a status symbol, particularly when returning to the cooler duller climates of northern Europe. It has remained so up to the present day, although acquiring a suntan has become far less exclusive.

With the establishment of the short, straight silhouette, many fashion conscious women tried to achieve a completely flat shape. Foundation garments like a modified corset were designed to deliberately flatten the breasts. A few women even bound their breasts. *Punch* showed a drawing of two thin, flat-chested women. One is complimenting the other enthusiastically, 'My dear, you have got absolutely nothing'. The ideal for the fashionable figure had changed completely from the 1900s when rigid corsets were designed to exaggerate every curve of the well covered female form. The typical 1920s woman had arrived and clothes had become simpler and scantier than anything people could have imagined even five years earlier when many women thought they had already reached the ultimate in modern practical clothes. Comparing illustrations in fashion magazines for 1910 and 1925, the change is very great and must be amongst the fastest and most revolutionary in the history of fashion.

The very simple dress shapes with a plain straight across neckline, no sleeves and two side seams, were easy to make. Some women were able to run up basic slip-style dresses in a variety of fabrics at home quickly and cheaply. With the difficult economic circumstances many families experienced, home dressmaking was the only way many women could afford to dress their families. Some women developed their making-up skills and became quite accomplished dressmakers and were able to supplement the family income by dressmaking for friends and acquaintances.

Better off women had their clothes made by professional tailors and dressmakers or bought them ready to wear from the fashion departments of the big stores.

The most exclusive place for women to buy their clothes was still the couture fashion houses where the clothes were expertly fitted and made and the designs were always several months in advance of the other areas of the fashion market.

During the middle of the decade Oxford undergraduates started to wear wide flapping trousers known as 'Oxford bags'.

Younger men started to wear far less formal clothes. Baggy 'plus fours' were worn with fancy patterned pullovers and matching long socks.

At the weekends modern young people got away from the towns, like this daring couple boating on their own.

Britain still ruled a vast Empire, middle-class men's stores like Austin Reed's had special tropical kit departments.

With the simple, modern, more sophisticated style of dress, the girlish flirty, early post-war flappers began to be replaced by a more worldly type of woman who was often rather blasé and superficial with a brittle manner. Words like 'darling' and 'angel' were scattered randomly among quite casual acquaintances rather than being reserved for loved ones. Quite ordinary objects were often described as 'divine' or 'heavenly'. Many of the women in Noel Coward's plays were rather like this and well known stage personalities such as Gertrude Lawrence and Talulla Bankhead typified the new modern woman.

Chanel became a famous designer during the twenties and established herself as an important and lasting influence on 20th-century fashion. Like Poiret during the late 1900s she caught the changing mood of the time. She believed clothes should be more functional and allow for greater ease of movement. Her sleeves, bodices and skirts were all cut to give this freedom without being unnecessarily loose or baggy. Clothes were cut to flatter the figure without emphasising it. This was often achieved by cutting on the cross of the material which gave the maximum suppleness and ease. She popularised the use of knitted fabrics, particularly jersey which previously had been used mainly for vests and underpants. Chanel styled the fabric into easy fitting but well cut jackets, skirts and dresses. When English woollens and tweeds were used she put fewer and softer interlinings so that the garments looked lighter and less constructed. Her clothes tended to make women look younger and slimmer.

Chanel helped change the way status was shown through dress. The old ideas of intricately made garments in rich fabrics with plenty of surface decoration, although greatly modified, did linger on into the early twenties and were slightly reinforced by the attempts to revive more ornate fashions. By the mid twenties the fashion lead had been firmly taken by the younger Paris designers such as Chanel, Molyneux and Jean Patou with their very simple

The Chanel influence is shown clearly in these resort clothes of the late twenties. The uncluttered blazer jacket and cardigan suit were typical of the more understated way fashionable women were dressing.

clothes in plain materials and colours such as beige, navy and grey. Elegant understatement became the new more subtle hallmark of being well dressed and the more discreet way of showing affluence. Far less jewellery was worn. Long dangling earrings, rows of beads and too many bracelets on the arms and round the wrists was now considered rather vulgar and ostentatious. It became smart to wear simple stud earrings in gold or pearl with a single row of pearls round the neck. One or two bracelets with a matching brooch or a single bracelet worn on the upper arm was also popular. Items in fake or semi-precious stones were chosen and admired for design rather than value. Chanel liked this costume jewellery and had it made for herself, helping its popularity.

Fashionable women aimed to look neat and uncluttered. 'Chic' became a popular way of describing clothes that were on a higher plane than styles that were just in the latest fashion. Chic clothes had to have some extra special flair in the cut, the use of fabrics, the colours, or a combination of all three. Fashion leaders such as Lady Edwina Mountbatten and Mrs Daisy Fellows were known for wearing outfits that had this flair and they were often described as looking very chic. The clever, individual choice of clothes and the way they were worn was also part of looking chic. Having a tailored blazer jacket made in an evening fabric such as

Swimming costumes, like in this Ovaltine advertisement, were functional.

Deep cloche hats were worn even with functional ski outfits.

Briefer swimming costumes and sunbathing became popular.

Short casual hair styles worn by mother and daughters. The mother's hair is slightly longer and softer but many young women wore the same short flat cut as the young girls. The little girls' party dresses on the right are miniature versions of the women's fashions with their flat low-waisted bodice.

satin or clustered sequins to wear over a flimsy evening dress rather than wearing the usual evening wrap, or wearing cheap cotton trousers and a sailor top on board ship or in a resort, were examples of the new approach to clothes.

Wearing a jacket or a coat pulled round the shoulders with the sleeves hanging loose is supposed to have originated with Chanel feeling cold one evening on board the Duke of Westminster's yacht. She borrowed a man's jacket and because it was too large put it casually on her shoulders and unwittingly started a way of wearing jackets and coats that was to be copied by countless women.

With the simple, straight up and down line, accessories were more important. Gloves in suede or soft leather were still always worn or carried in winter or summer. Rather medieval gauntlet shapes with soft folds round the wrists and flaring out slightly up the lower arm were sometimes pulled over the narrower sleeves of dresses and jackets and made the main feature of some outfits. Square shape handbags with longish handles looked rather large and too prominent with the new very short skirts. Smaller oblong bags in soft calf or shiny patent leather, either squashy looking with fancy clasp fastenings or flat clip down envelope shapes, some with initials embossed on the flap and held in the hand or pushed under the arm, looked neater and in better proportion with the new silhouette.

For a woman to have well-shaped legs became more of an asset than ever before. Stockings and shoes were very important. Black stockings which had been generally worn were now replaced by flesh coloured ones in silk or cotton lisle. Silk stockings were expensive but considered worthwhile for town and evening wear. For the country and sportswear such as golf, ribbed and patterned woollen and cotton stockings were usually worn. Diamond patterns in the traditional Argyle or based on the Argyle designs were very fashionable for women and men. In the summer, light-coloured cotton ankle socks were quite popular.

Town shoes were neat looking and fairly simple in design. Lizard and crocodile skins were admired but expensive. Suede and polished leather was more generally worn. Basic styles were lace-ups or court shoes with slightly pointed toes and medium and high heels, either Louis shaped or straight cut. Black, navy and brown were worn in the winter; for the summer, white, beige, pale grey or two-tone effects such as beige or white with toe and heel caps in navy or brown. Shoes with a single or T-strap fastening across the foot were also very popular and are often considered very characteristic of the 1920s. Long boots like a slightly squashed down riding boot and called 'Russian' boots were a fashion craze in the mid-twenties but only for a few years and they were never as widely or continuously worn as the high boots of the sixties and seventies.

Although more practical shoes were worn in the country and for casual and sports wear, it was considered important to have the correct and fashionable styles and for shoes to be neat and well polished. Informal shoes had round toes and lower heels which were either cuban shaped or flat and square. Top stitching or the use of brogue was greatly used on toe and heel caps. Most shoes fastened with laces or straps. Some styles were rather open over the arch of the foot and laced across before being tied. These were called 'gillie' shoes and were based on traditional Scottish styles.

Evening shapes and designs were similar to the everyday town shoes but made in dressier fabrics such as satin or brocade and often dyed to match evening dresses. Silver and gold kid was also greatly worn and was very versatile in teaming up with a wide variety of dresses in different fabrics and colours. Fancy bows were sometimes used on the front of shoes. Buckles in silver or diamanté were also used as decoration or as part of the strap fastening.

The revolutionary fashion changes of the twenties eventually affected the way most women dressed. Only the elderly stuck to modified versions of the styles that had been fashionable in the early part of the century. Queen Mary was an example of an older woman who continued to wear the styles of the early 1910s. She never adopted short hair, cloche hats and low-waisted skimpy dresses. Her style of dress always remained the same; long hair waved and curled onto the top of the head, draped toque hats trimmed with feathers, and ankle-length tailored clothes and dresses that followed the curves of the bust, waist and hips.

It was the upper and middle class youngish women who eagerly followed the fashion changes and wore the latest hats and dresses within months of their introduction. Less well off women had to follow fashion more slowly and cautiously. They tried to present a neat and tidy appearance and chose quiet, safe designs that wouldn't date too quickly and they only gradually shortened their hair styles and skirt lengths. Moderately-priced mass-produced clothes were improving, especially in America where there was an established clothing industry catering for a wide market. But class distinction through dress was still quite marked, particularly in Europe.

Poorer people looked more obviously poor, with shabby clothes in low quality fabrics. Their aim was to be adequately dressed; fashion hardly came into it. Many women still had unmade-up faces and pulled their hair into a knot or chopped it off into a rather plain, flat-looking cut. They wore plain pull-on hats with few trimmings for everyday wear but tried to keep a better hat for Sundays or special occasions.

A lot of men, women and children were poorly shod. Working class men and boys usually wore unfashionable lace-up boots and their wives and sisters had to wear what they could get in the way of footwear. Their shoes were sometimes bought secondhand or as children's feet grew, shoes were handed on to the younger members of the family. The differences in the quality and stylishness of people's clothes were far more noticeable than during the later decades of the century.

During the mid and late twenties deep-crowned cloche hats pulled down to the eyebrows and shaped onto the nape of the neck were almost universally worn.

The changes in men's fashions during the 1920s were not as fast or revolutionary as the changes in women's dress but they were fairly radical and more fundamental than in the 1900s and 1910s. Men were as anxious as women to forget about the past and get on with the new post-war era. Their changing attitudes began to be reflected in a gradual move away from formal and over-disciplined clothes to a more casual way of dressing. The younger generation led the way and started wearing far less formal clothes on holiday, at the weekend and for general wear at universities and colleges.

Fancy patterned pullovers in crossway checks or traditional Scottish Fair Isle designs, often home knitted by fond mothers or girlfriends, were worn instead of waistcoats with tweed suits

Town shoes were neat looking and fairly simple in design. Lizard, crocodile and python skins were used, but too expensive for many women.

The woman drawn in the cigarette advertisement typified the rather artificial looks of the later twenties – deep suntan, pencilled eyebrows and bright red 'rosebud' mouth.

or sports coats. Baggy knickerbockers, called 'plus fours', were very popular and were worn with long socks, sometimes in the same pattern or edged with the same pattern as the pullovers. The flat-shaped cap or a soft pull-on hat completed the outfits. The Prince of Wales liked these sort of clothes and was frequently photographed wearing them, particularly on the golf course.

Men's trouser shapes were still quite narrow in the leg at the beginning of the twenties but younger men began to prefer easier, baggy trousers. Towards the middle of the decade, Oxford under-graduates started to wear exaggeratedly wide flapping trousers known as 'Oxford bags'. Interest was now focused on the legs for both sexes; very short skirts for women and extremely wide trousers for men. Oxford bags had a limited success and did not last very long but their influence persisted and within a few years most men's trousers were cut loose and fairly wide with pleats at the waist. This cut lasted for a long time. With the easy widish trousers, simple flat-heeled lace-up shoes in brown or black leather, known as 'Oxfords', became the basic everyday shoe for most men. Apart from active sportswear, boots were not liked by the younger generation, perhaps because of their associations with uniforms and the war years. Boots were now usually worn only by older men.

Stiff collared shirts and rather stiff-looking single-breasted suit jackets with matching waistcoats were still worn by many men but with the looser trousers, easier fitting jackets, double-breasted without waistcoats or single-breasted over a short double-breasted waistcoat and worn with softer shirts with longish pointed collars were popular with fashion conscious younger men.

Hair styles were as short as ever and like the women's Eton crop, frequently rubbed with oil or cream to flatten the hair and make it look even shorter and neater. The back of some men's heads had an almost eel-like appearance. If a man's hair grew on the neck it was shaved off. These styles were certainly not flattering to men with prominent ears or irregular features. Some young men grew their hair longer on the top while keeping the short back and sides. The front hair fell slightly over one eye, the head being tossed back when it fell too far forward. This became a familiar gesture of many undergraduates and young men in the twenties and thirties.

Most men still wore hats. Bowlers or Homburgs were nearly always worn with conventional business suits, and gloves were important accessories. With the new more casual clothes men started going without hats or wearing one of the more informal 'trilby' shapes which were in soft felt dinted down through the middle of the crown, turned up at the back and pulled down at the front at a slightly rakish angle. Some men spent quite a lot of time before going out trying to decide on the best and most flattering angle to wear their hats.

In England the young generation of men who had been too young to fight in the war were now grown up and included a great deal of talent in the literary and artistic world. Evelyn Waugh, Cecil Beaton and Noel Coward were amongst this bright generation. They had their own mannerisms and style of dressing. They had various affectations in the way they spoke. They would emphasise certain words for effect or their speech would be clipped or staccato or lazy and drawly. The sort of clothes they liked included monogrammed silk shirts, patterned silk cravats worn inside open-necked shirts, roll-necked pullovers and pale grey flannel trousers worn with suede shoes. Noel Coward was famous for his printed silk dressing gowns and was often photographed lounging on a sofa in a silk dressing gown looking rather bored and smoking through a cigarette holder. Their preferences in behaviour and dress seem fairly moderate by later standards but they were criticised and viewed with suspicion by many people who had very conformist ideas of men's clothes and thought it was a sign of being effeminate for a man to wear even slightly different styles of dress or show too much interest in fashion – very different from the flamboyant men's styles of the sixties which were so easily accepted, particularly in England.

Although the 1920s saw a gradual move away from a rigid conformity in men's clothes, it was a slow development. There were well accepted ideas on how a man should dress. It was part of everyday routine for middle and upper class men to change from their business suits or day outfits into evening dress. Dinner jackets were worn for informal occasions such as dining at home or in restaurants, attending concerts and theatres and going on to one of the new noisy night clubs. For formal dinners and dances stiff white shirts with stand-up collars, white ties, gloves and cut-away black tailcoats and matching black trousers were always worn.

The adoption of more casual styles made the greatest impact in the clothes worn for the growing popularity of active leisure pursuits. At the weekend, the younger generation began to break away from the old idea of wearing formal Sunday best clothes to go for a sedate walk after church. Instead they went to the country or to the seaside. Motorbikes were becoming increasingly popular and the riders needed a certain amount of protective clothing. Men, and some daring young women, wore outfits rather like the early aviators; leather jackets, gauntlet gloves and leather helmets were worn with plus fours or riding breeches. Walking and hiking were an inexpensive way of seeing and enjoying the country. Practical outfits were a necessity. Berets or simple pull-on hats were worn with roomy sweaters and baggy shorts or plus fours which were teamed up with long woollen socks and tough lace-up shoes. Men and women wore similar clothes but some women wore pleated or divided skirts instead of trousers or shorts.

This picture of the famous Dolly Sisters in their fringed dresses captures the 'dance mad' mood of the twenties.

Rudolph Valentino in his costume for his best known film *The Sheik*. He was an adored fantasy man for thousands of women.

Clara Bow known as the 'it' girl epitomised the emancipated young woman of the time.

Both sexes wore fairly covered up swimming costumes but they were becoming briefer.
They were usually sleeveless with a round or straight across neckline in the front and scooped
out at the back. Some more advanced styles had bare backs and were held up with straps
which crossed over from the shoulders to the waist. Legs were less covered. The trouser part
of the costume finished at least three or four inches above the knee.

Children's clothes benefited from the simple easy fitting approach to dress. Girls wore
shorter miniature versions of women's fashions that allowed them to enjoy far more freedom
and ease of movement. The long tumbling curls so much admired in the previous decade
were now cut to a short manageable length. Straight hair was cut in a neat flat page-boy
style, ear or chin length with a straight across the forehead fringe. Hair was not layered and
on some girls it looked rather plain and unflattering and was sometimes called a
'pudding-basin cut'. Deep cloche hats, almost identical to women's styles were nearly always
worn when going out, particularly in Town. Girls were expected to be very neat and tidy with
gloves and long stockings or socks and well-polished shoes.

Boys also enjoyed wearing versions of the new casual grown-up styles during the holidays.
Tweedy caps and fancy patterned pullovers with rather baggy short trousers were worn by
young boys; older boys wore plus fours or wide trousers and greased back their hair. During
term time, school uniforms were still rigidly adhered to. Hair had to be kept very short.
School caps were always worn when out of doors. Apart from active sports wear, collars and
ties were worn and boys wearing short trousers had to keep their long school socks neat and
straight. Failure to present the correct appearance was not tolerated.

Mass entertainment reached a far wider audience than ever before during this period.
Radios and gramophones were increasing every year and an industry developed producing
and promoting popular dance music. Young people were thought to be 'dance mad'. They
danced at home, at afternoon tea dances and in the evening in dance halls. Some danced on
into the early hours of the morning in night clubs. The Prince of Wales was known to enjoy
night club life and the smart London clubs he frequented such as the Embassy and the Kit
Kat Club became internationally known. Evening dresses with their low waisted fringed or
glitter embroidered bodices and flounced or loose panelled skirts suited perfectly the
fashionable dances such as the 'Shimmy', the 'Charleston' and the 'Black Bottom' with their
shaking, jerking movements.

The cinema also attracted an ever-growing following. The fantasy world of romance and
drama offered a wonderful escapism for many people, particularly the more deprived. The
film stars' looks and their style of dressing became a major influence. The two extremes of the
'vamps' or the rather sugary sweetness of the good girls began to be replaced by a wider range
of heroines. Modern girls with made-up faces and fashionable clothes who enjoyed a good
time without being too sophisticated or too wicked appealed to many young men and women.
Clara Bow, known as the 'it' girl, epitomised emancipated young women of the time. Her
type 'had it all', all the admired characteristics. Joan Crawford, who was to become so famous
during the following two decades, started to be featured in films during the latter half of the
twenties. Her early roles such as the one she played in *Our Dancing Daughters* cast her as a
flirty modern young woman. In one scene she dances a Charleston demonstration on a night-
club table surrounded by admiring young men.

Many ordinary women of the time copied the hair styles, make-up and clothes of the film

A quieter more serious dress for autumn 1929. The waist is back in its natural place, the skirt is slightly longer, and the falling hemline is emphasised with two longer back panels.

stars rather than trying to imitate in a modified form the more ladylike styles of the middle and upper classes. They found the film star fashions enabled them to be noticed and shine a little more in their own social circle.

Male film stars were admired at least as much as the female stars. They were usually cast as dashing heroes in period costume, smouldering with passion and ready to sweep young girls off their feet. Rudolph Valentino literally did this in many of his acting roles, pulling a bewildered protesting girl on to his horse and galloping off across the plains or deserts. The admiration for Valentino with his Latin good looks was phenomenal. He was an adored

Two 1928 evening dresses. The fashionable silhouette was softening waists (much nearer to the natural waist) and skirts which dipped to the ankles at the back.

fantasy man for thousands of women all over the world and was sometimes referred to as the Prince of Sex. When he died in his early thirties in 1926 there were scenes of mass grief and hysteria at his funeral in New York.

Fashion and music are social reflections of the time and register a change of mood before most people are aware of the changing times. This certainly seems to have been so during the late twenties when popular music and clothes were softening and becoming more wistful as if anticipating the end of the party and the more serious times ahead.

As early as the autumn of 1927 the hard angular silhouette was showing signs of slightly softening. Dresses were still flat chested and low waisted but there were more necklines with draped scarf collars. Bodices often crossed over and tied with a floppy bow on one hip. Designers were showing longer fuller skirts, particularly for the evening. The longer look was achieved with uneven hemlines rather than a definite all round drop in length. Dresses had dipping points, flowing panels or transparent over-skirts a few inches longer than the under-skirt, or were knee length in the front and dipped almost to the ankles at the back. This style was surprisingly popular.

The new softer lines affected everyday clothes much more slowly. Women liked the simple practical clothes they had adopted and they were in no hurry to give up their Chanel-inspired jersey suits, loose straight coats or versatile blazer jackets which they found suited their more active life.

During 1928 and 1929 the more feminine look began to develop more noticeably. Women grew their hair longer and although neat and flat looking it was waved back and rolled tightly across the nape of the neck or allowed to fall into tidy curls at the back. The bare-necked shingle and Eton crop gradually lost favour. Hats were still deep and helmet shaped

Evening dresses from the autumn collections in 1929. The fashion lines of the early thirties have already arrived with slim hips and long droopy skirts.

but less uniform in style. Crowns were often draped and brims were turned a little further back to show more of the forehead and hairline and then dipped at the front or sides.

The natural curves of the figure remained unemphasised but were no longer flattened and the slight shape of the breasts and waist showed again. Waistlines were still low but nearer to the natural place. Because women were so used to very low waists, dresses with slightly higher belts were described in magazines as high-waisted. Sleeves were fuller, flared at the cuffs or full shirt sleeves gathered into a band at the wrists and called 'Bishop sleeves'. Skirts fitted round the hips but then gradually flared and were quite full round the hem.

The Paris autumn collections for 1929 confirmed the new more feminine silhouette. Waists were back in their natural place. Skirts were calf length for day and ankle or floor length for the evening. Soft lines were featured even for suits and coats. Suit jackets were shorter and sometimes belted. Skirts were flared or had unpressed pleats. Fur collars and cuffs were still popular on coats but cape effects round the shoulders and styles that flared out towards the hem gave a very feminine look to the autumn designs. Dresses were often cut completely on the cross of the fabric giving a flowing rather droopy line that looked its best on women with slim hips and long legs. Slender hips and thighs were very important. All the new styles emphasised this part of the figure.

Clothes had become quieter, more mature but less positive than the typical 1920 fashions of a few years earlier. The Wall Street crash in October 1929 triggered off the slump and the great Depression. A more sombre period was starting and the predominant fashion lines of the early 1930s were ready and waiting by the end of 1929.

The
1930s

The Depression: colours were dark, hats, hair styles
and necklines all dropped downwards.

Revivals and interest in earlier periods continue throughout the history of fashion. During the
20th century, perhaps because of the bewildering changes in everyday life and the insecurities
caused by World Wars and political changes, nostalgia for the recent past of twenty to forty
years before has been a recurring theme. From the late 1950s onwards, nostalgia for the
1930s has been particularly strong and enduring. This prospect would have been very
surprising to people during the thirties or for the first fifteen or so years after the end of the
decade because in many ways it was a troubled and serious period that started with an
economic depression and ended with another World War. The fascination for the decade
may lie in its split character. Many of the political and economic problems are still unresolved
and therefore easily identified with by later generations. But the other side of the thirties
character with its light-hearted escapism and stylishly elegant way of life ended with the
Second World War and seems to have been permanently lost in the social changes of recent
decades.

For the women who could afford them, the fashions of the early thirties were certainly
stylish and elegant. The longer more flowing lines that had been featured in the Paris
collections in the autumn of 1929 were strongly reconfirmed by the fashion world in 1930 but
it took a year or two for some women to take up the new styles. The worsening economic
situation meant many women simply could not afford new clothes. Brave attempts were made
to bring their outdated short-skirted styles into fashion by adding bands of contrasting
material or fur round the hemlines. The added fabrics were also sometimes put round the
end of the sleeves or made into scarf collars so that the overall effect looked really designed
rather than an after-thought. Other women resisted the new styles at first because they felt
they were retrograde and unsuited to the more modern way of life.

However, within a couple of seasons the new fashions were firmly established and definite
style characteristics had emerged. All the fashion lines, as if reflecting the slump, drooped
downwards. Longer hair was waved lower onto the nape of the neck. Hats were either skull
caps with draped folds at the sides and back, or modified cloches with brims that dipped
down over one eye. Necklines were cut to fall into rather monastic-looking cowls, and
shoulders looked very sloping with soft cape effects. Sleeves had low fullness from the elbows
to the wrists where they were loosely draped into cuffs or floppily tied. Skirts were long and
lean looking, gradually flaring into low unpressed pleats or godets which were triangular
pieces of material stitched into the skirt seams so that they flopped rather limply when a
woman walked. Day skirt lengths fell to the bottom of the calf.

Colours and fabrics also reflected the subdued mood of the early thirties. Black, navy and grey were basic everyday town colours. Browns and greens were popular for autumn and winter country clothes. Afternoon and evening dresses were usually in black or powdery pastel shades which ranged from pinky beiges and peach to eau-de-Nil greens, greys and soft blues. To suit the new cut in clothes, fabrics were draped and floppy, fine wools, crepe and jersey for day clothes, silk chiffon, crêpe de Chine and soft shiny satin for evening dresses.

With the establishment of more elegant and ladylike fashions, the older woman was admired again and the girlish flappers in their teens and twenties were no longer the fashion ideal. This suited some of the ageing flappers quite well. They were getting into their thirties and found the new longer flowing lines definitely more flattering. Although the older woman was back in fashion, she was expected to have kept her figure and have narrow boyishly-slim

Backless bodices and floor length back sweeping skirts were a feature of evening dresses during the early thirties.

Fashion became more elegant, and the slightly older woman was admired. She was expected to have kept her figure and have narrow boyishly slim hips.

hips. Women dieted more seriously than ever. A famous saying of the time was 'A woman could never be too thin or too rich'.

One of the new fashion ideas of the early thirties was that there could be a distinctively different length for day and evening clothes. When shorter skirts came in during the First World War and through the ups and downs of hemlines in the twenties, day and evening lengths were about the same. With the more realistic mood caused by the Depression, day clothes had to remain a fairly practical length even with the adoption of the elongated silhouette, but for the evening there was no reason why they couldn't be long and flowing. Floor-length evening dresses were worn again for the first time since the early 1910s. This compromise suited the escapist side of the thirties character. Women were able to change from their neat day clothes into gorgeously impractical evening dresses. Evening-dress styles quickly developed along rather theatrical lines. Period costume presented a fairly limitless source for ideas but unlike the attempts to revive costume effects in the early twenties, the 1930s revivals didn't bother to relate too closely to the everyday silhouette. Once the practical limitations of day clothes had been divorced from evening wear the scope for fantasy was wide open.

A well-off fashionable woman might dress one evening in a Grecian outfit, a draped dress with a gold belt and sandals and an appropriate Grecian-looking hair style. A few evenings later she could wear a frilly Victorian-style dress with puff sleeves and a hair style to match the period of the dress, either arranged in ringlet curls or parted in the middle and pulled into a bun at the back. The same fashion-conscious woman might have appeared for another occasion in a sophisticated black velvet and taffeta cape and rustling evening dress inspired by the Paris fashions of the late 19th-century.

Backless evening dresses were a daring new innovation in the early thirties. The back was

Elegant outfits for watching polo in 1931. The men are also immaculately dressed in wide topped white breeches and polished polo boots.

cut out almost to the waistline. The material for the front part of the bodice was taken from the side seams near the waist and crossed or draped up over the breasts and was held or fastened round the neck like a halter. The skirts of these dresses were usually cut on the cross of the material, clinging to the hips and flaring out to touch or trail on the ground like a softer modified version of the skirts worn during the 1900s. Backless dresses looked sensational on suntanned young women with good figures. In the opening scene of Noel Coward's *Private Lives*, Amanda, played by Gertrude Lawrence, stood on a hotel balcony with her back to the audience. She was very suntanned and wore a clingy backless white crepe dress designed by Molyneux. A gasp of admiration is supposed to have come from the audience.

Although most women did not wear the more extreme styles, evening dress fashions were very popular and women who could afford them enjoyed the growing variety of designs. The middle classes with secure jobs lived well during the Depression years. Prices fell and quite ordinary suburban homes had maids. Many middle-class women had several new evening dresses for each season, summer and winter, so that they were not seen too often in the same dress. Evening dress was always worn for the theatre in provincial towns and cities as well as the capital until the beginning of the Second World War.

As well as the separate developments in day and evening clothes, other areas of fashion became more categorised. Women were expected to consider carefully the suitability of clothes for different occasions and the time of day. Neat coats, suits and dresses were correct until after lunch when progressively more dressy outfits were worn, particularly for early evening cocktail parties. For special occasions such as weddings, garden parties and fashionable race meetings, outfits consisting of large floppy hats fussily trimmed and long trailing dresses more covered up but similar to evening dresses in length and shape were worn. They were called Ascot dresses. England's fashionable Ascot race meetings were the perfect place to show off clothes, weather permitting. Some women appeared in a different Ascot dress each day and spent a considerable amount of time and money on their eye-catching outfits. Although Ascot was revived again after the Second World War, the post-war styles have usually been dressier versions of everyday clothes or publicity-seeking eccentricities. The special Ascot-style dresses have never been revived.

For attending less formal sports occasions during the thirties women wore what the fashion magazines described as 'spectator sports clothes'. In the spring and autumn, jaunty looking day suits and coats in flecked tweeds or checks worn with fairly plain hats and shoes were the right type of clothes to wear for watching golf tournaments or point-to-point horse racing. In the summer, navy blazer jackets teamed with cream or white pleated skirts, simple colour matching hats and two-tone shoes, or day-length printed silk or cotton dresses and straw hats would have been the appropriate clothes for attending polo games or for watching tennis matches. Several successful wholesale fashion houses called themselves Spectator Sports or specialists in Spectator Sportswear.

Specially designed clothes to wear on the popular ships cruises or in holiday resorts came into their own during the early part of the decade. In the morning if a woman was not engaged in some form of active sports, she wore simplified versions of town suits and dresses, usually made in white or pale-coloured linen and sometimes braided in a contrasting colour, particularly navy on white with its nautical look. The nautical theme was often emphasised with motifs such as anchors or ships' wheels embroidered on the pockets or reveres of suits

The younger members of the British Royal Family, the Prince of Wales shown here with Mrs. Simpson, were often photographed in casual resort clothes.

Ascot 1931. Large floppy hat and long trailing dress similar in length and shape to many of the evening dress styles.

and dresses. More informal and functional clothes were worn for deck games on board ship or on the beaches in the resorts. Longish, fairly wide shorts and low-backed halter necked tops were popular with the growing passion for sunbathing. A beach jacket was usually worn over the sun top and a button-through skirt over the shorts for the journey from the cabin to the deck or from the hotel to the beach. Although many women thought they were modern and emancipated, they were still quite modest about showing too much of their bodies in public compared to the later generations.

Trousers had been worn by the more advanced fashion conscious women in the late twenties but they were more generally adopted in the early thirties. Flapping bell-bottom trousers and loose tops known as 'beach pyjamas' were a craze that soon became over popularised. Well chosen resort wear with colourful accessories were a welcome development that looked their best on young women with good figures but vulgarised versions of the new styles were soon worn, and cartoons of rather brazen-looking women in beach pyjamas or sun tops and shorts soon appeared in newspapers and magazines. They usually showed overweight women waddling down a promenade, sitting on the back of a motorbike or bending over on the beach. Rude looking seaside postcards often date from this period and are still reprinted today in the summer clothes of the thirties.

A smart couple dressed in their 'tennis whites'. Women's day skirts were calf length but tennis dresses, like this one, were well above the knee.

Although rather quaint by today's standards, swimwear became more recognisably modern and began to be better fitting. The one-piece costume made in elasticated fabrics started to be worn. They were cut like the bodices of evening dresses with low backs and halter necklines. Slim girls photographed in them were often described as 'streamlines' – a popular word during the thirties, used to describe something modern and progressive. During the middle of the decade two-piece swimming costumes began to make their early appearances. The tops were cut like a longish bra and the bottom halves covered the seat and the top of the legs quite modestly but they caused a stir at the swimming pools and on the beaches. Aspiring young film or stage actresses were photographed for newspapers and magazines, pertly posed in their 'two pieces'. This has continued through the decades as the tops and bottoms have become progressivley smaller until the top halves disappeared altogether on some beaches.

Resort clothes were soon an established part of summer dressing. Members of the British Royal Family, the Prince of Wales and the Duke and Duchess of Kent were often photographed on a beach or on board ship wearing very casual holiday clothes.

With the growing popularity of active sports, appropriate sportswear was designed to cater for the functional needs of the sport rather than modifying basic day styles. There was still an influence from the fashionable silhouette but it was far less than in the early decades. Although day dresses were longer, tennis and skating dresses were shorter than they had ever been, well above the knee and pleated or flared to allow for maximum movement. Movement was also important for golf clothes. Golf skirts had especially deep pleats and many women started to wear loose mannish tailored trousers, usually called 'slacks' and waterproof

Very stylish high fashion resort wear in 1933. Modern young men and women were wearing the same cut in jackets, trousers and shorts.

Swimwear became more recognisably modern – costumes fitted better and the two-piece began to be worn.

functional jackets. Apart from special events and certain hunts when some women still rode side-saddle, most women were riding astride and wore almost identical riding clothes to those worn by men – similar hats, shirts with ties, and masculine tailored tweed or twill hacking jackets, and wide-topped riding breeches or jodhpurs in Bedford cord or cavalry twill. Breeches were worn with long boots; ankle boots went with jodhpurs. Jodhpurs were slightly more popular with women; the fabric shaped to show the curves of the legs looked a little softer and more feminine. Skiing holidays continued to grow in popularity and became an annual event for many of the more prosperous classes. More attention was paid to special ski wear. Basic ski clothes consisted of weatherproof caps, matching jackets and baggy trousers tucked into socks and rather basic lace-up ski boots. Magazines showed ski clothes in their early winter issues and there were slight variations in colours and styling, but in retrospect they appeared rather dull and lacking in imagination. Ski wear was to develop more excitingly than any other form of sportswear during the later decades of the century.

Keeping fit and looking healthy became a great preoccupation. Many young women wanted to look sporty and suntanned and develop or keep a good figure. Figure trimming exercises were illustrated in magazines with detailed photographs or drawings of the correct movements. The exercises were practiced at home or in groups at 'health and beauty' classes where women could do their exercises under supervision with a piano playing one of the popular songs in the background 'Keep young and Beautiful if you want to be Loved'.

The new mature fashions and the more categorised ways of dressing changed the kind of clothes the more prosperous classes wore but for the vast numbers of people who experienced the adverse economic conditions with reduced living standards or unemployment, the world of fashionable clothes was less attainable than ever. Many women had to make their clothes last longer. They renovated and altered whenever possible. Hats were retrimmed or had their shapes changed. Different collars were put on to dresses and home dressmaking became more popular than ever. The styles of the early thirties were more complicated to make and required more material than the short straight lines of the twenties but resourceful women turned out suits and dresses with the new lines and managed to look up-to-date for a comparatively small outlay of money. Home knitting also thrived. Women's magazines carried regular illustrations of pullovers, dresses and accessories with detailed instructions for knitting. During a period when so many women had to be extremely thrifty, home-knitted items helped to brighten up their everyday clothes.

Simple basic types of clothes such as knitwear or blouses with skirts and button-through shirt style dresses became the practical garments many women wore for several years. A different belt or scarf and a new hair style helped women who had to follow fashion changes at a very modest and homely level.

The selection of mass-produced clothes continued to improve. Many women admired and hankered after the smart clothes displayed in the shop windows but had little money to buy them. When clothes were bought, practical serviceable styles were usually chosen. The elegant high-fashion styles shown in magazines like *Vogue* were only worn by a small minority.

By 1933 and 1934 fashion lines were becoming less droopy looking. Hair styles were still neatly waved and curled but there was a growing tendency to take them upwards. The upswept hair styles looked better with the wide range of new hat shapes. Hats had broken

By 1934 fashion had become less droopy. The two Schiaparelli designs show the new built up shoulder line.

away completely from the uniformity of the cloche hat. There were many small hat styles; popular shapes included pill boxes, flat berets and fezs, lightly trimmed with feather and veiling, and worn tilted forward or to one side. For dressy and formal occasions, especially in the summer, quite large hats were often worn. They had shallow crowns and flat brims and were usually tilted forward and frequently had an elastic band attached to the inside of the crown. The band was pulled over the back of the head to hold the hat on and in position. With the more elaborate hair styles the elastic band was often cleverly concealed amongst the waves and curls.

Coats, suits and day dresses were cut on neater, more precise lines. Shoulder width began to be emphasised for the first time since the beginning of the century. Sleeves and bodices were more shaped and fitted. Collars and revers on coats and suits fastened higher up and the revers pointed upwards towards the shoulders rather than drooping down. The newer cut had a slightly military look.

Fur coats reflected the military influence with stand-up collars and turned back cuffs. A flatter pile fur was more suitable for the newer styling and fit. Soft curly Persian lamb became very fashionable. Full-length coats and jackets were too expensive for many women; Persian lamb as a trimming was widely used for collars and cuffs, whole sleeves, muffs and pillbox hats. Silver fox was another extremely fashionable fur also greatly used for trimmings and hats. Rather bulky looking elbow or hip length capes in silver fox were very much admired and sought after. They gave a wide and yet soft and flattering look to the top of the long, slightly more shaped silhouette.

A fox or a pair of foxes were frequently worn as accessories. They were wrapped around the arms, draped over the shoulder, or a single fox was put on one shoulder, the head hung down the front and the rest of the fox complete with tail was taken over the shoulder, across the back and fastened at the side; the head clipped on to the tail and formed a lasso-shaped loop across the body. Dangling fierce looking foxes' heads with glass eyes filled restaurants and theatres to the horror or amusement of small children.

By the mid-thirties designers were thoroughly enjoying the more or less unlimited scope for evening dress ideas. Styles varied widely even in the same designer's collection. Ideas from historic costume became ever more popular and sometimes quite authentic looking with the return to more figure-emphasised curves. Designers in their search for ideas jumped happily from decade to decade and century to century, often mixing the periods up at will; even the recent past of the early 1910s was successfully revived with hip drapery and flaring tunic tops.

As evening dresses became increasingly extravagant, many women felt they could only be worn for really special occasions. Something was needed for comparatively informal evenings. The gap in evening wear was filled by a new category – dinner dresses. Dinner dresses were ankle or floor length but more related to day dress styling than the extravagant evening dresses. They usually had sleeves and some had high necklines which must have been welcome to women in the winter. Many homes still had no central heating, particularly in the English country. Dinner dresses often had matching jackets varying in length from short boleros to hip length tunics. Sometimes the design features of the dresses, the gathered sleeve heads or sequin-embroidered motifs, were repeated on the matching jackets.

One of the best known designers of the 1930s was Schiaparelli. She did much to promote the livelier more varied fashions most women were wearing by the mid thirties. She was one of the first designers to feature the wide built-up shoulder line. Perhaps she was inspired by her Italian heritage and the puffed out sleeve heads of the Renaissance. Her designs certainly had a dash and a swagger about them that was very different from the quiet elegance of designers such as Chanel and Molyneux. Schiaparelli was less concerned with subtle under-statement and the evolution of cut. Her designs were far more extrovert. She used her Italian colour sense for bold and unusual combinations of colour such as emerald green with bright blue, or strong cerise pink which became known as Schiaparelli's 'shocking pink' teamed with navy or black. Schiaparelli knew many of the famous modern artists of the period. Some of the striking embroideries used on her jacket and dress bodices were clearly inspired by the fashionable surrealistic art of the time. As well as influences from modern art, many of her fashion collections had slightly crazy themes featuring circuses or rather theatrical military or police-style uniforms. These lively, rather light-hearted fashions were very ahead of their time and really came into their own with the fantasy clothes of the 1960s.

Some of Schiaparelli's design ideas seem to have verged on the publicity-seeking kind of novelty such as her hats that looked like a dangling sock or an inverted shoe, or her suits and dresses that were fastened with buttons shaped into hearts or lips. But her flair for novel and controversial design ideas helped bring an element of much needed fun after the rather subdued fashions worn during the early years of the decade.

The couture fashion houses were still the most exclusive places for women to buy their clothes. With the growth of the wholesale garment industry, chain stores and the more expensive department stores came into their own. Fashion buyers had to be very knowledgeable about fabrics and the way garments were made. They also had to be extremely fashion conscious. They went to the Paris fashion shows twice a year to absorb the latest trends. They then adapted the new lines with the wholesale manufacturers so that women were able to buy clothes in the most up-to-date styles from the stores almost as quickly as the original designs could be made in the workrooms of the couture houses for individual customers. Women who were not affected by the slump had more opportunity to be

Well cut suits and coats with the wider shoulder line, shaped waists and
slightly shorter skirts were popular in the later thirties.

This Jean Patou evening dress, with full sleeves and wider flaring skirt, was influenced by the styles of the
1890s.

Adrian, one of the best known Hollywood dress designers, created this
sophisticated black wool suit for Joan Crawford.

fashionably dressed than ever before and the differences in the styles worn by the classes
began to narrow.

Apart from fashionable clothes, the big department stores catered extensively for women's
interests and needs in one building. Departments ranged from basic household goods to
jewellery. Costume jewellery in semi-precious or fake stones having been accepted and become
fashionable in the twenties, became even more popular during the thirties. Jewellery
departments were quite extensive. The designs of costume jewellery were more sophisticated
to suit the more feminine style of clothes. Rhinestone and *diamanté* earrings and clips were
very fashionable and were usually designed to be worn together or separately. The earrings
were stud or heart shaped and the clips were often larger versions of the same shapes. They
were worn fastened to scarves or collars and were sometimes worn in pairs on the necklines of
dresses. One was clipped on each side to pull the neck open and down so that it formed a
diamond or heart shape. Dresses were described as having 'sweetheart' necklines.

With the more elaborate evening-dress styles which often had sleeves or drapery over the
shoulders and the top of the arms, interest was focused on the dress and there was less room
or need to add as much decorative jewellery. Bangles and bracelets were less popular but
necklaces were sometimes worn. High pearl chokers were revived. They complemented the
period costume look of many of the dress styles.

Any lingering resistance to obvious cosmetics and dyed hair had gone by the mid thirties.
Make-up was heavy by later standards but more skillfully applied than during the previous
decade. Women's magazines were full of instructions and tips on applying it. Faces were often
covered with a rather thick foundation called 'pancake' make-up. It looked rather like a
pancake mix. Once the foundation make-up was on, the rest of the face was filled in.

Marlene Dietrich at her most glamorous in the veiled hat and fox fur she wore in the 1936 film *Desire*.

Hollywood musicals epitomised the escapism of the time. Fred Astaire and Ginger Rogers danced their way through many light-hearted films.

Make-up was heavy by later standards but more skilfully applied. Lips became more emphasised.

Eyebrows were drawn on, eyelids and lashes shaded and the face was dusted with powder. Cheeks were still rouged but more discreetly than during the twenties and the little 'Cupid bow' mouths were no longer fashionable. Mouths were made to look as large as possible. If a woman felt hers was too small she deliberately enlarged it and filled it in with dark red lipstick. The large red mouth became the most emphasised part of face make-up.

Make-up and hair dye were used to imitate the rather artificial and impressive looks of the film stars. Blond hair was greatly admired, sought after and fairly attainable. Hollywood film studios must have got through substantial quantities of dye. Potential film stars' grooming usually began with bleaching their hair. If they were already blond they became blonder. White blond, known as 'platinum' blond was the pinnacle of blondness. Jean Harlow, one of the most famous sex symbols of the decade, was known as 'The Platinum Blond'. Some women peroxided their hair at home. The peroxide was put in a saucer and then brushed into the hair, sometimes with an old toothbrush, the hair being parted and rebrushed until the desired effect was achieved. Some dyed heads looked rather crude and brassy. Detrimental remarks were sometimes made about the looks of 'peroxide blondes'.

The cinema was at the height of its popularity during the mid to late thirties. Women and quite a lot of men were very influenced by the looks, clothes and behaviour of the film stars. People went to the cinema regularly, sometimes several times a week. New cinemas were opened all over the world and older ones were rebuilt on grander more impressive lines. Some of these buildings are now considered to be of historic and architectural interest. They were certainly shrines to the great influence films exerted in the thirties. Cinema-going represented escapism on a mass scale. People could at least watch the portrayal of the stylish and elegant way of life even if they had no chance of participating in it. The lavish Hollywood musical epitomised the escapism of the time. Fred Astaire and Ginger Rogers danced their way through many light-hearted musical romances and Busby Barclay's ingenious and spectacular musical sequences have become cinema classics. He featured clever and unusual themes. The high spot of one film was an elaborate set with multiple rows of pretty girls playing white grand pianos. In another film, scores of girls dived into an enormous swimming pool where they formed complicated flower patterns. In *Gold Diggers of 1935*, the Lullaby of Broadway scenes involved hundreds of film extras and many different sets. In the frantic dance routines Busby Barclay seemed to capture the rather desperate good-timing of the period.

The clothes worn in American films possibly had a wider influence on the way women dressed than the Paris couture fashion shows. Although Paris set the new fashion lines, Hollywood quickly adapted them for their film stars and women all over the world copied the clothes they liked on their favourite stars.

Some individually talented dress designers worked for the major film studios. Adrian was one of the best known. Although he geared his clothes to the needs of the cinema, they were as original and creative as many of the French couture designs. Adrian helped popularise wide padded shoulders. He was supposed to have thought of the idea for Joan Crawford, one of the most successful box office stars. She was reputed to have been rather broad hipped for the very slim lines of the time. Adrian built out the shoulder lines of her outfits and made her hips appear more slender. Other women soon discovered it could do the same for their figures. This may have been one of the reasons padded shoulders remained in fashion for so many years.

Children's clothes followed some of the newer
developments in cut and style in a simplified form,
but hair continued to be short and neat.

Greta Garbo and Marlene Dietrich were two of the most admired superstars of the thirties.
Garbo's face was unforgettably beautiful and classical but her wide shouldered, lanky
Scandinavian figure might not have been so admired in other decades. She suited the clothes
of the period, the tailored suits and coats and particularly belted trench coats worn with dark
glasses and a beret or a floppy brimmed hat. Hats like the one she wore became known as
'Garbo' hats. The softer side of the thirties fashions, drapey blouses and dresses, also looked
very appealing on her. She was supposed to have felt intuitively about the clothes she wanted
to wear. Her style certainly made a lasting impression. Many women today still wear trench
coats with dark glasses, have their hair medium length and uncontrived looking and generally
follow the style Garbo made famous over forty years ago.

'Glamorous' was a word that started to be used in the thirties to describe attractive women's
looks. Marlene Dietrich might have invented glamour. It certainly became synonymous with
her name. Glamour was warmer and sexier than chic and elegance in women's looks but it
was still slightly aloof. Glamorous became very descriptive of the way the fashions in women's
looks and clothes were developing and becoming more alluring, feminine and figure
conscious. Marlene Dietrich was usually cast as a sophisticated *femme fatale*. Her clothes were
dressy looking but not fussy. She wore flattering hats trimmed with fur or veiling. Her suits
and coats were immaculately tailored without being too masculine. Sumptuous furs were
often draped casually around her shoulders and although skirts were longish, she usually
managed to show her fabulous legs through slits or with a slight hitch up of her skirt when
she sat down.

Apart from the looks and the clothes worn in films, the type of woman portrayed had an
influence on women's mannerisms and behaviour. The restless flighty flappers in the films of

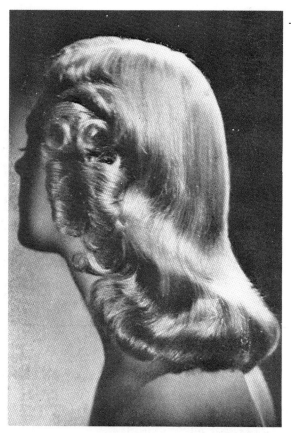

In the later thirties, long hair was waved down and turned under on the shoulders. 'Long bobs' were copied from the American film stars' styles.

Hair swept on to the top of the head and pinned into curls was called the 'Edwardian style'.

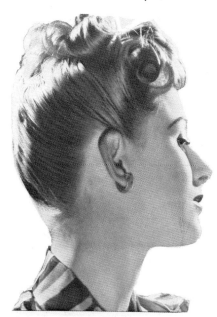

My mother in the late thirties – longer hair and fashionable silver fox cape. The photograph of her on p.60 is taken ten years earlier with the less flattering Eton Crop.

Shoe styles were cut with high decorated fronts. Scottie dogs were very popular and appeared regularly in photographs and drawings.

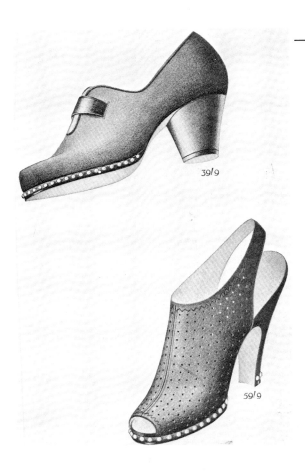

39/9

59/9

Platform soled shoes with varying shaped heels were a new fashion of the late thirties.

the twenties who sometimes appeared to have been suffering from over-active thyroid glands were very out of date by the mid thirties – the new modern type of woman was more cynical.

The fashions shown in the films, like the ones in the magazines, were still out of reach for many women. The economic situation gradually improved during the second half of the decade but it was a painfully slow process and as the depression in industry began to lift the threat of war started to grow.

Some of the younger generation were very politically conscious. Their political convictions were more obvious than the earlier social reformers, and showed in their dress. Many of them were quite anti-fashion even though some of them came from affluent backgrounds. Because of the serious world problems, they felt time and money spent on their appearance was unnecessarily frivolous. The clothes they wore were basic and functional. Hair styles for women were straight, uncontrived looking and chopped off at the chin or the shoulder, or long and pulled into a bun or pinned up in plaits. Men had short hair but it was often longer and less groomed than was usual for the thirties. Although many young people went hatless, berets were occasionally worn and girls sometimes covered their heads with scarves tied at the back or under the chin like peasants' head scarves. Both sexes wore similar everyday clothes. Basic looking jackets with open-necked shirts or roll-necked pullovers and baggy unpressed corduroy trousers with plain lace-up shoes or sandals.

Despite anti-fashion attitudes and the worsening international situation, fashion continued to change and develop new silhouettes. Between 1936 and 1938 new lines emerged.

Hair was worn much longer and women had plenty of scope to arrange it in many ways. Young women liked the American film star styles which were parted at the side or in the centre, and waved or curled onto the shoulders, or the front and sides of the hair were pinned up and the back was left long and loose or turned under on the shoulder like a long page-boy style. These kind of hair styles were called 'long bobs' and became increasingly popular. Versions of them have been worn in all the decades since the thirties. More sophisticated hair styles were swept up onto the top of the head and pinned into elaborate rolls or curls and were described in fashion magazines as 'Victorian' or 'Edwardian'. They were really showing an influence from these periods rather than a total revival.

Fashionable women became very hat conscious. Hats were an important and noticeable part of their outfits. Autumn and winter styles were based on rather mannish shapes with high crowns. Tyrolean-looking hats trimmed with feathers and softened with veiling were very fashionable. Late 18th-century and Regency men's styles were also adapted for women. They had curled or shovel-fronted brims and were tilted onto the forehead and turned up at the back to show the waved or rolled hair styles. The high crowns were usually trimmed with a toning or contrasting band of ribbon which was sometimes pulled through a large buckle in the front and emphasised the Regency influence. Shiny straw was greatly used for summer hats. They were usually fairly large saucer shapes and trimmed with artificial flowers or fruit and worn tilted sideways at a rather drunken angle.

The fashionable silhouette changed; it became less elongated. The established broad shouldered lines became even more exaggerated. Tailored suits and coats had square box shaped shoulders; softer suits and dresses, padded out gathered sleeve heads. Even blouses, knitwear and dressing gowns had shoulder pads. The curves of the figure were clearly emphasised. Clothes were more shaped over the bust line and trimly fitted into the waist. Very narrow hips were no longer so important. Hip emphasis was revived with softly flaring tunic jackets, draped dresses and gathered skirts. There were more skirt shapes ranging from very narrow styles with front or side slits to gathered, pleated or flared designs. Skirt lengths were shortened slightly each year and by the autumn of 1937 they were upper calf length and noticeably shorter.

The return to figure emphasising clothes and the revival of more womanly and alluring fashions during the second half of the thirties developed strongly in 1937 and 1938. Any trace of boyishness or hard looking chic was completely out of date. Fashion began to return to the modified form of the long despised curves and ultra femininity of the first decade of the century.

With the more feminine and varied clothes fashionable women needed a wider range of appropriate accessories. Gloves were very important and had to be carefully chosen to suit the outfits. For sophisticated town clothes wrist gauntlet and elbow-length gloves were worn, either in suede or soft kid. Expensive gloves had decorative features. The edges of gauntlet shapes were sometimes scalloped, or the slightly flared upper part of the glove was patterned with tiny eyelet holes or embroidery. Simpler short gloves in leather or wool and combinations of the two were worn with country clothes. Knitted gloves in fancy patterings were popular with the many women who knitted at home.

Fashion-conscious women frequently changed their handbags several times a day. Small neat handbags continued to be fashionable particularly with afternoon and evening dresses but as the day silhouette became fuller and more elaborate, larger bags were re-introduced. Very soft leather or suede was used for dressy-looking styles which were draped or gathered into quite prominent fancy roll or clasp fastenings. Many of the styles had broad strap handles and they were draped or pleated to echo the design feature of the bags. Summer handbags were sometimes made in linen to match suits or dresses and they were appliqued with colourful flower or abstract designs.

Upper-class men always changed in to evening dress,
even for bachelor evenings at their clubs.

Men's suits had a broader look. Shoulders and revers
were wider, trousers were cut loose and straight from
the waistline to turned up cuffs.

There were many new shoe styles. Town shoes were dressier and more sophisticated
looking. Suede was greatly used. Shapes varied – more delicate looking styles had almond-
shaped toes and medium or high straight heels. Many of the designs were high cut and laced
over the arch of the foot with silk or fancy cord laces. Delicate bows and draped silk bands
were also used over the high fronts and there were plenty of decorative effects on the heel and
toe caps including rows of top stitching or very narrow strips of leather on suede or suede on
leather shoes. Some afternoon and evening styles had cut out holes like a stencil pattern
decorating the fronts or sides.

As an alternative to the dressy kind of shoes, different heights of heel and shapes of toes
were introduced. They were chunkier looking with lower broader heels and round or square
toes. The design details were simplified versions of the ones used on the more delicate high-
heeled shoe styles or they had turn-back fronts like the turn-back flaps on golf shoes. Many
women liked the more practical lower-heeled styles. They were suitable for the town or the
country and busy day-to-day lives.

Strappy open-toed sandals became a basic style during the decade. Sandals with Cuban or
flat heels were worn with resort clothes and summer dresses. High heeled more delicate styles
in suede or soft kid were often worn with afternoon and evening dresses. Some women wore
them with their everyday suits and coats. Leading fashion magazines with their set views on
the selection of appropriate accessories did not approve and declared fussy open-toed shoes to

Hair was still worn very short, but more men were beginning to favour natural unoiled styles like Errol Flynn's hair in 1938.

Popular male film stars of the thirties, like Tyrone Power, were neatly turned out with conventional clothes.

be in bad taste when worn with tailored clothes. Despite the disapproval of the fashion oracles, open-toed and sling-back shoes became even more popular during the late thirties and the styles were more frivolous. Some had platform soles and wedge heels.

A parallel development in shoe designs took place. The designs were ultra practical and clumpy. They had broad toes which were wide and round or squared off and snub fronted. Heels were flat and heavy looking or shallow wedge heels were joined up with thick platform soles. 'Nothing is dowdier than a dainty foot'. *Vogue* commented in 1939. Perhaps it was a good thing the fashion promoters thought that because most women were likely to have few opportunities to wear dainty shoes during the following six or seven years.

Dogs were often used as a kind of fashion accessory during the thirties. Women's magazines included them in their fashion drawings. Famous personalities were photographed with their favourite dogs and dogs were featured in films. Terriers were the most fashionable. 'Asta', the wired haired terrier in the famous Thin Man films had an audience following that many of the human film actors and actresses must have envied. But the most popular of all the terriers was the Scottish terrier. As well as the Scotties in fashion drawings, *Vogue* always headed its Shop Hound pages with drawings of Scotties running off with a spring hat or in the autumn issues muffled up with a tartan scarf. There were cotton prints featuring Scottish terriers as a motif and the revers of suits and coats were sometimes decorated with a Scottie brooch.

Children's clothes continued to have easy fitting simple lines. Girls' outfits looked less like miniature versions of women's fashions. The more sophisticated figure emphasising grown-up styles didn't suit young girls' looks or figures. Girls' dresses were based on the loosish lines of the twenties but were slightly influenced by the style details of the thirties. Sleeve heads were often gathered or puffed out and normal waistlines were marked with a belt or a material tie. Dresses cut like a long button-through shirt became a basic style, long sleeved in the winter and short sleeved and made in lighter materials for the summer. Shirt dresses with slight variations have remained a standard dress style right up to the present day.

Girls' top coats followed in a simplified form some of the newer developments in cut and style. Although they were quite easy fitting, they were shaped to follow the general lines of the body; they were higher fastening and trimmed with braiding or they had velvet collars and cuffs. These kind of coats became very characteristic of the period and remained a children's fashion style until the 1950s.

During the 1920s, mothers and daughters frequently had the same simple short flat looking hair-cut. In the thirties girls' hair styles continued to be either short and neat or long and plaited. Mothers indulged in the new upswept curls and rolls. When girls left school and started work in shops or offices there was a fairly quick transformation from schoolgirl clothes and school uniforms to grown-up womanly fashions, make-up and fancy hair styles.

A 1937 wedding group. The bride and bridesmaids all have puffed out sleeve heads on their dresses.

The eve of the Second World War, 1 September 1939, and the neo-Victorian rival adapted for the wholesale market — rounded bust and shaped waist.

The Paris fashions in 1938 promoted the return to the hour-glass and modified versions of the Edwardian styles.

The looser roomier men's clothes that had been liked by the young generation in the twenties developed into the basic lines of all men's clothes during the thirties.

A broader built type of man's figure, wide shouldered and athletic looking, was admired in most countries. The growing power of the mass media, particularly the radio and the cinema, helped create a kind of national hero worship for film stars, sportsmen and in Fascist Italy and Germany stern faced warriors in sinisterly smart uniforms.

Hollywood, shrewdly sensing the changing mood and the re-establishment of more overtly masculine images, made less films featuring the Latin gigolo type of man or romantic sensitive heroes. War films that had been considered so uncommercial during the twenties became popular. The leading men often played dashing aeroplane pilots wearing tough-looking leather helmets and battered flying jackets. The men portrayed in gangster films were less obviously good looking than the earlier film stars but more earthy and masculine. The descriptions of them became part of the slang of the time. They were called 'tough guys', 'he men' or 'the strong silent type'. Some of these descriptions are still used today.

Many young men tried to impress their girlfriends by looking as much like one of the tougher film stars as possible. They wore long, loose raincoats or overcoats with the collars turned up over double-breasted navy or grey chalk-striped flannel suits and completed the

Hats were tilted forward and the rolled hair styles were sometimes covered with wide hairnets called 'snoods'.

gangster look with a wide brimmed soft hat dipped down at the front and known as a 'Snap Brimmed Trilby'. It was a rather over-slick way of dressing that was heavily influenced by the George Raft type of film actor.

Most men's clothes were less exaggerated than the ones worn by the film stars but they were broad looking. Overcoats and raincoats were wide shouldered and cut full in the body and sleeves. They had large collars and revers and like the women's lengths, they were well below the knee. Suit jackets were also square shouldered and had big revers. They shaped slighty in at the waist but were cut straight and flat over the hips, again similar in shape to the women's silhouette. Trousers hung loose and quite wide from generously pleated waistlines to turned up cuffs. Turn-ups were worn on all everyday trousers.

The quiet understated English style of dressing continued to be admired by many men. The fashionable silhouette was modified by the more exclusive tailors. Shoulders and revers were only moderately wide. Colours and fabric patterns were more subtle.

The rules for the correct clothes to wear for all occasions were still followed and taken very seriously. In case they were unsure or badly informed, men's magazines laid the details out clearly. In a 1938 man's magazine, *Style Guide*, a double page was set out, sectioned and tabulated with all the details of men's clothes to cover all possible occasions. In the same magazine there is a paragraph on correct evening wear: 'For dining at the club, the privacy of one's own family circle, for dinner at home with personal friends, aboard the *Queen Mary* or any other first class liner, for smoking concerts and a happy bachelor evening, the dinner jacket, single-breasted or double-breasted coat, is strictly correct. Occasionally it may be worn at one of those small informal dinner parties in the Grill Room but although this is permitted it is regarded as too informal and not sufficiently dignified for the place and the occasion.'

The accessories in men's fashions changed less than the basic lines. Hair was still very short and often greased back although more men were beginning to favour natural un-oiled hair styles, slightly longer and wavy or floppy on top. Most men still wore hats but the softer Trilby shapes were much more widely worn even with business suits and coats.

Shoe styles continued to be mainly plain and conformist. Flat heeled lace-ups with toe and heel caps in black or brown leather was the only style worn by many men. Design variations were very limited. Rows of stitching or brogueing were occasionally used, and golf and country shoes were rounder and sturdier looking. Two-colour summer shoes with navy or brown toe and heel caps on white shoes or loafer and moccasin slip-on styles and shoes with a single strap fastening called 'Monk' shoes were sometimes worn, particularly in America, but they were considered far too conspicuous by many men.

Undergarments for men usually included baggy underpants and vests. Elastic suspenders that crossed over the legs and clipped onto the socks to hold them up like women's suspenders were habitually worn by some men and could not have done much for the shape of their legs. Many shirts still had detachable stiff or semi-stiff collars that had to be held on to the neckband with a stud. Shirt sleeves were quite full and were held above the elbows with wide elastic bands. Although sports trousers sometimes had belted waistlines, most trousers were held up with braces and hitched up high at the back. Unless they were very well cut the fit over the seat was baggy with unnecessary folds.

The fashionable broad cut in men's wear was not right for the proportions of boy's figures until they were in their late teens. Younger boys, like the girls of the time, continued to wear the simple easy lines that had been established during the previous decade, particularly during the holidays. In the summer, everyday clothes consisted of short-sleeved shirts, school blazers, pullovers and short or long trousers. Boys up to the age of twelve or thirteen usually wore short widish trousers which ended two or three inches above the knee and were belted into the waist with an elastic belt which was sometimes in striped school colours. Older boys wore wide long trousers with turn-ups. Boys and girls usually wore T-strap fastening sandals in tan leather with crêpe soles. Clarks, the English shoe manufacturers, were famous for their children's sandals.

School uniforms were still rigorously enforced in private schools. Parents were presented with detailed lists of the required items of clothing ranging from underwear to top coats. Children who attended State schools were not expected to have such elaborate uniforms but they had to present a neat and conventional appearance and if possible wear blazers and a school uniform type of outfit.

Despite the setbacks and hardships many people experienced during the 1930s, American influences grew. Popular dance music, stage shows and Hollywood films were followed and copied all over the world.

By the late thirties the Depression was lifting and a new energy and vitality was

The
1930s

Fashion fads are forgotten and young couples are parted as the men go off to war.

regenerating the American way of life. With the growing threat of war in Europe and the Orient, America became a good place to be, and it's renewed self-confidence began to be reflected in both music and dress. Well styled mass-produced clothes at all price levels enabled American women to have up-to-date fashions even if they had quite modest incomes. Visitors from Europe were impressed by the stylishness of the young women who worked in offices and shops. The slickness of their hair styles, make-up and clothes were at a higher level than most of the women in Europe who worked in similar jobs.

American influences dominated popular music. The jerky jazz and softly sentimental tunes of the late twenties and early thirties was replaced by the well organised and highly professional big swing bands. Swing music with its brash lively rhythms or smooth flowing ballads seemed to express America's more confident mood. Ballroom dancing was at the peak of its popularity. Dance floors were filled with women in pretty evening dresses and sprucely-dressed men in black evening suits guiding them through the long striding dance steps of the foxtrot, the quick-step and the waltz.

The band leaders were as well known as the film stars. Glenn Miller and Tommy Dorsey were mobbed by their excited fans on their successful tours across the States. There were several off-shoots from commercial swing music – Latin American rhythms introduced new dances, particularly the rhumba with its hip swaying movements. Dancing the rhumba presented a good opportunity to draw attention to the figure-fitting evening dresses with their softly draped hip lines. America's young generation wanted even more exuberant music and dancing. Jive and boogie-woogie provided an outlet for their energies. They waved their fingers and arms, twirled partners around and the really energetic indulged in minor acrobatics. Girls were thrown over the boys' shoulders or between their legs. It was called 'jitterbugging'. Young people had their own style of dress for jitterbug competitions. Girls wore blouses or sweaters and short flared or pleated skirts with white socks and gym shoes. They were often called 'Bobby Soxers'. The boys wore loose sweaters and baggy trousers.

They had their own slang. They listened to their favourite bands at 'Jam Sessions'. If they knew a lot about the music they were called 'Hep Cats' and they followed the progress of a new record in the 'Happy Cat Hit Parade'. America was very advanced with its teenage cults. It was the beginning of the many youth cults that were to follow the Second World War.

The Paris fashion designers in 1938 seemed to have accepted the view of many of the politicians that appeasement would prevent another World War. Their new designs were very unsuitable for women about to be involved in a war that would effect civilians more seriously than ever before.

The Paris collections promoted the return to the hour-glass figure with a pulled in waist. Modernised corsets were introduced to help achieve the new shape. *Vogue* advised its readers, 'Where there is a will there is a waist'. Fashion seemed to be going back to the beginning of the century. Hair was piled on top of the head in revived Pompadour styles. Hats were fussily trimmed and tilted forward. The bodices of suits and dresses fitted tightly over the breasts and rib cage and the pulled-in waist was made to look even smaller with strongly emphasised hip lines. Jackets curved out over the flared skirts and dresses were draped out at the sides or up at the back to give a bustle effect. In the Paris fashion shows for autumn 1939 Balenciaga, one of the new designers of the late thirties, showed some dresses with built out width at the sides and although day skirts were getting shorter, he showed longer lengths to balance the wide proportions. Rich Victorian colours were revived; dark purple, plum, wine shades and dark greens and blues. Fabrics were also deep and rich looking. Bouclé wools and velvet were popular for dressy day clothes; taffeta and corded silks suited the wide skirted evening dresses.

Most women were not ready for the rather fanciful neo-Victorian designs; only the very fashion conscious wore them. Modified versions were more generally worn or women took up part of the new style such as a fussy-looking doll hat, a more fitted suit or a full-skirted afternoon or evening dress.

While the high-fashion dress designers were becoming rather carried away with their somewhat impractical ideas, functional clothes were developing in the background. Wide hairnets called 'snoods' helped to keep long hair neat and out of the way. Headscarves instead of hats were becoming increasingly popular and were tied round the head like a turban. Mannish tailored jackets worn with pleated skirts or trousers became safe basic items for many women. There were many clumpy shoe styles and although the fashionable silhouette was figure fitting, day skirt lengths continued to get shorter. By 1939 most women were wearing a practical just below the knee length. Fashion seemed to have been assembling its own Territorial Army in case it was needed.

When the war started these more practical clothes became the basic styles women were going to wear for the next six years. In the closing months of 1939 functional war clothes became familiar in most European countries. Steel helmets and military caps replaced men's hats on hall stands. Fathers appeared in uniform and families from babies to grandparents were fitted out with gas masks. The return to ultra femininity had to be postponed until after the war when it was to be successfully revived with Dior's famous 'New Look'.

The 1940s

The 1940's was a unique decade in 20th-century fashion. The effects of the Second World War had made fashion less exclusive and clothes became more democratic, catering for a much wider market.

At the beginning of 1940, although the European war had been on for several months, extensive bombing and fighting had not started. In France, fashion designers were given special leave from the Armed Forces to complete their new collections. The couture houses presented their spring fashions in February to an international audience in an atmosphere of 'business as usual'. The American press, who had expected to report sensational war news, called this period 'The Phoney War'.

The fashions for 1940 were more practical than the frivolous styles of 1939 but they were still designed for women whose lives had not been too affected by the war.

Hair styles continued to feature pinned up curls and rolls. Hats were surprisingly fussy; there were two main shapes – forward tilted doll hats and newer looking bonnet or boater styles worn on the back of the head. Most of the designs were delicately trimmed with ribbons, flowers and veiling.

The basic silhouette of the late thirties continued with wide shoulders and figure-fitting lines, but the tiny corseted waistlines that had been considered so important only a season before were quietly forgotten. Some designers were showing easier-fitting bodices cut like a man's shirt. Clothes had become more wearable, design details were simpler and there were less outfits designed for special occasions. All day skirt lengths were shortened to just below the kneecap, but for the evening floor-length dresses were still shown. In *Vogue's* report on the collections it was noted that 'Women are dining gracefully again in dresses that touch their toes'.

In May 1940, Germany began the invasion of Holland, Belgium and France. The 'Phoney War' was over. By the end of June France was defeated and Paris as the international centre of fashion had to close down.

Paris under the German Occupation was completely cut off from Britain and America. The couture houses lost a very important part of their market but they showed small collections throughout the war years and fashionable dressing was still seen. Smart restaurants were busy and social events including some of the well known race meetings continued to take place.

The fashion houses managed to produce elegant clothes despite the difficult conditions but it was not possible for them to introduce new silhouettes. They based their designs on the established lines of 1940 with practical but stylish additions. Winter top coats had attached hoods, fur linings and matching fur-lined ankle boots to cope with the cold streets and unheated buildings. Big pockets were made a fashion feature on coats and jackets and they were large enough to hold some of the scarce items women were always on the lookout for

As well as the special practical ideas of the fashion designers, most women had to adapt their way of dressing to the changed circumstances. Because of the acute shortage of transport, short full skirts were worn by the many women who took up cycling. During the summer, girls with curls piled on top of their heads or loose flowing hairstyles cycled in girlish-looking dresses showing knees and thighs.

Leather shoes became extremely difficult to obtain. Shoes had to be made with heavy

Autumn 1940 – fashions were still designed for women whose lives had not been too affected by war.

There were more women in uniform than ever before. Womens caps, shirts and tunics were almost identical to those worn in the men's services.

The Duchess of Kent in WREN uniform.

War-time weddings were simpler, men in uniforms and women in short day dresses.

wooden soles and wedge heels. Resourceful women refused to accept the ugly appearance of these shoes. They decided if the soles and heels had to be so prominent they would make a feature of them, like Dutch clogs. They painted them in bright colours, sometimes in contrasting layers of stripes or they decorated the sides of the soles and heels with studs or small shells.

Hats was the area of fashion where startlingly new styles were adopted. Huge turbans became very characteristic of French women during the occupation. The turbans varied from expertly draped couture designs trimmed with flowers and smothered in veiling, to cheeky home-made concoctions in plaited straw or coloured paper. Towering turbans became a kind of symbol of French women's determination to follow fashion and keep their independent spirit alive. They flaunted their crazy looking hats despite disapproval of the authorities and their undisciplined headgear contrasted cleverly with the dull grey caps worn by the women in the occupying forces who the French called 'the grey mice'.

The Second World War affected civilian life far more than the 1914-18 War. Many parts of Europe and the Orient were severely bombed. Food and consumer goods were scarce and often strictly rationed. The pre-war pace of fashion changes stopped but women's interest in make-up, hair styles and clothes continued and many women managed to look attractive and well dressed even in the countries that were severely involved in the war.

German and Austrian women are often portrayed in British and American films set in the

In London's fashionable Bond Street two women talking wear more functional clothes – turbans, flat shoes and trousers.

war years as dowdily dressed and heavily built. Some women, particularly the Berliners and the Viennese, had a long standing reputation for elegant and fashionable dressing. This continued right through the Nazi period and women lucky enough to have husbands or boyfriends stationed in Paris sometimes received clothes or accessories as presents. These items, with their obvious French 'chic', stood out in the home atmosphere of rationing and restrictions.

The shared affects of total war unified Britain and made the nation committed to the war effort. Everyone, male or female, rich or poor, young or old, had to carry a new accessory slung on one shoulder – gas masks in gas mask holders. There were more women in uniform than ever before. Unmarried young women were conscripted into one of the three Services or the Land Army, or they were directed into the armament factories. Married women with children over 14 years old also had to undertake some form of compulsory war work.

Women's uniforms for all ranks in the Services consisted of the same basic types of garments: military caps, shirts and ties, tunic jackets with matching skirts, thickish stockings and flat lace-up shoes. Officers' uniforms were slightly smarter. They had better shaped caps and their uniforms were well cut and made from quality fabrics. Some officers wore wide polished leather belts round the waists of their tunics, similar to the men's Sam Brown belts. Uniform colours were the same as in the men's Services; khaki, Air Force blue, and dark navy for the WRENS, the Naval section. WREN uniforms were often thought to be the smartest and some young women liked the uniform so much they made considerable efforts to get into the Naval service.

Women in the Forces had to use make-up discreetly and hair styles had to be neat and kept off uniform collars. Off-duty, heavier make-up was used and girls literally let their hair down for parties and dances. Long waves and curls bounced on uniformed shoulders as girls jived to hit records like Glenn Miller's *In the Mood*.

There were less opportunities for the Land Girls, the girls in the Land Army, to enjoy a sophisticated off-duty life. Land Girls wore their own kind of uniform – plain pull-on hats or berets, shirts and ties, pullovers, baggy corduroy riding breeches and long woollen socks with sturdy lace-up shoes.

Women who were not in the Services but worked on day or night shifts in factories went to work in plain functional civilian clothes that tended to give a drab appearance. Box-shaped jackets and coats were worn with trousers or skirts and zip-fronted ankle or calf-length boots. Most women wore headscarves which were tied under the chin or wrapped round the head and tied in front like flat looking turbans. Many factories made it compulsory for women to cover their heads with scarves to prevent hair getting caught in the machinery.

Rows of women in turbans and overalls singing popular songs, *Roll Out the Barrel* or *Don't Fence Me In* at factory canteens' 'Workers' Playtimes', were typical of the surprisingly cheerful spirit of women who worked unsociable hours in noisy factories and also had to put up with bombing and rationing as part of their everyday lives.

Women of all ages and classes whose lives were constantly affected by air raids wore trouser outfits. Special all-in-one boiler suits called 'siren suits' were worn by women and children in the air-raid shelters. In the winter, knitted head and neck covering Balaclava helmets and knitted gloves were worn and a suitcase with a change of clothing for the family was taken into the shelter in case the home was destroyed during the air-raid.

Nearly all consumer goods were rationed. It was the fairest way of trying to ensure everyone had some of the limited resources that were available. Generally, rationing in Britain was well planned and efficiently run. Clothes and fabrics were rationed from 1941 onwards. Everyone was issued with an annual number of coupons, the total number varying with the general availability of clothing and materials. The smallest annual issues were made in the later war years. Every item of clothing from overcoats to handerkerchieves had an allocated coupon value. A suit or top coat took a high percentage of the total allocation leaving few coupons over for basic items such as underwear or stockings. The replacement of clothes had to be carefully planned. Laddered stockings sometimes came as quite a disaster. Precious coupons would have been needed for new ones even if they could have been found. Some women painted their legs with make-up or coffee and because real stockings were always seamed, imitation seams were drawn up the back of the legs with an eyebrow pencil by a helpful friend or relative. If the painted legs were unexpectedly caught in the rain they became embarassingly streaky and dirty looking.

Women took great care of their clothes to make them last. Newspapers and magazines carried regular articles called 'Make Do and Mend' on how to alter and renovate existing clothes. Dyeing garments another colour or trimming or re-trimming them were the easiest ways to revive interest in clothes that had become boringly familiar. Tailors and some clever women managed to make women's outfits from men's suits. Dinner jackets and trousers were

Above: Regulations were introduced to control the materials and styles used for some clothes – they were marked with the utility symbol. *Below*: Cycling was the method by which many women travelled around. Casual knitted tops were worn with padded square shoulders.

Practical summer dresses. The girl with the lifted hairstyle and built-up sleeves was the slightly more fashion-conscious of the two.

a popular choice for conversion. Many men were away from home in the Forces and were not likely to miss their civilian evening clothes. The jacket and trousers were completely unpicked and pressed flat. A woman's jacket and skirt were then re-cut from the material.

Material lengths and knitting wools were on coupons and sometimes in short supply but many women preferred to make their own clothes. Fashion magazines gave more space to knitting patterns and styles for the home dressmaker. The thin issues of *Vogue* always had attached pattern books. Women found they could make clothes with more style and individuality than the rather stereotyped designs in the shops, particularly when manufactured clothes became subject to extensive regulations.

Regulations were introduced that limited the quality and the amount of material allowed for every type of garment, even the number of pockets and the amount of buttons were restricted. They were called 'utility clothes' and had a special utility symbol stitched into the back. To make sure clothes were available at prices most people could afford and to stop profiteering they were price controlled.

Well-known British couture designers including Norman Hartnell and Digby Morton designed special ranges of utility clothes for wholesale manufacturers. Fashion magazines showed photographs of the new designs and praised their simple, uncluttered lines. It was the beginning of well-known names in the fashion world designing for the mass market.

A certain amount of higher fashion clothes were still produced. These non-utility clothes were on coupons but they were free from style and fabric restriction and also from price control. Suits with wider revers, extra pockets and deeper pleated skirts or dresses with fuller sleeves and slightly draped skirts looked quite luxurious to women in the austere atmosphere of the time.

Utility or non-utility shoes were usually in short supply. When a shop got a delivery a queue quickly formed and the entire stock was usually sold out in a couple of hours. Shoe styles were clumpy looking with thickish soles and heels. Joyce shoes were very fashionable and became quite a prize possession. They were fairly simple, round-toed slip-on designs with small platform soles and moderately high wedge heels.

Stylish hats were very expensive but they were not rationed and women who could afford them had quite a wide range to choose from. Many of the designs were variations of the two basic shapes shown by the Paris designers in 1940, either small and pushed forward or larger hats worn on the back of the head. Newer looking designs were influenced by military headgear. Inflated looking berets were gathered into headbands and styles based on peaked caps had high fronts pleated into bands at the base of the crown.

Aage Thaarup was one of the best known milliners. He designed many of Queen Elizabeth's hats and his wholesale range was very much admired. Apart from fashion shops stocking his hats, he made personal appearances for a few days at certain stores and he created exclusive designs for individual customers. The client arrived for her pre-arranged appointment and was seated at a table surrounded by mirrors. Aage Thaarup then created the hat style on her head. Different shapes and angles were tried, fabrics were draped and several appropriate trimmings were considered before the final ones were selected.

Fashion-conscious hats were too expensive for many women but changing their hair styles helped to add some variety to their appearance. Fashion magazines tried to promote shorter styles. A few women, particularly in the Forces, cut their hair shorter but it was quite full looking and it was usually brushed upwards in waves or curls. Most women preferred to keep their hair long, enabling them to try several different styles. Long loose hair, turned under or waved onto the shoulders, was copied from the American film stars and was thought to be young and glamorous looking, but many women took their hair up for everyday wear. There were several popular styles; hair was piled on top of the head and held up with combs, or a band or a stocking was put round the crown of the head and the hair was swept over the band to form a continual roll right round the head. The style was called a 'Victory Roll'. It looked rather hard and severe on some women but was considered neat and practical and many women wore the style for several years.

Middle-class women with young children managed to lead comparatively normal lives. They had lunch and card parties and days out in town looking round the shops, had lunch in a restaurant and went to the theatre or the cinema in the afternoon. Although they had adopted more practical types of clothing they were always neatly dressed and for trips into the city or for Sports and Parents' Days they were smartly dressed in fashionable hats, tailored suits with matching or toning gloves, shoes and shoulder bags. Quite large shoulder bags with metal Army badges or Air Force wings attached to the flaps became a popular wartime

Clumpy shoes with wooden soles.

Joyce shoes were very fashionable and a new pair of 'Joyce Wedges' was quite a prized possession.

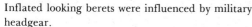

Inflated looking berets were influenced by military headgear.

accessory. The roomy bags were needed for the family ration books and identity cards.

In contrast to wartime Europe, America was a fashion Utopia where make-up, glamorous hair styles and stylish clothes were readily available. Well-established American couture designers such as Mainbocher and Hattie Carnegie were joined by Schiaparelli and many other European designers who evacuated to New York. Rich women had an even wider range of luxurious fashion collections to choose from.

Less well-off American women, particularly the New Yorkers, also reached an impressively high standard of dressing. The almost unlimited selection of moderately priced clothes and accessories enabled many women to dress like the illustrations in the fashion magazines. New York became the new international fashion centre and American women were the best dressed and the most envied in the world.

Fashionable make-up and hair styles were sometimes rather artificial looking and gave some women a hard almost varnished appearance. Make-up was heavily applied. Bright, glossy red lips and matching red finger and toe nails were the very noticeable make-up features of the time. Hair was often obviously dyed. Blond or red were the popular colours and hair styles were swept onto the top of the head and professionally arranged in neo-Edwardian-Pompadour styles, or worn down and smoothly turned under on the shoulders.

American clothes had very clean cut lines. The soft dressmaker styles of the thirties was

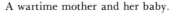

A wartime mother and her baby.

Aage Thaarup was one of the best known milliners.
He sometimes created exclusive designs for individual
customers.

considered old-fashioned. Suits and coats were sleekly tailored and made in smooth fabrics such as flannel or gabardine. Dresses and blouses were usually neat shirt styles with crisp looking collars and trimly belted waistlines.

Clear colours were popular, lemon yellow, creamy beiges, pale blues and bright pinks and reds. Black and navy were the smart town colours.

There were many sophisticated hat styles; large black halo hats were thought to be the most glamorous. They were made in brushed felt, velvet or shiny straw.

Black patent leather was very popular for shoulder bags and matching shoes. Patent leather shoes were made in dressy designs with peep toes and slingbacks. Platform soles and ankle straps were added to some styles. Film stars often wore these kind of shoes and they were much admired by deprived European women who saw them in American films but had no opportunity to buy them locally.

American *Vogue* and *Harper's Bazaar* were thick glossy magazines. They promoted the slick confident American style of dressing. Their fashion photographers were encouraged to take more casual less rigid looking pictures. There were many colour pages and resort clothes were photographed on location. This was quite a new and progressive development. Holidays were recommended in Argentina, Brazil and Mexico. The colourful clothes photographed in

American teenage girls wore rolled up jeans and ankle socks.

these exotic settings encouraged many Americans to travel greater distances for their vacations.

Latin America influenced a lot of the lively resort wear of the forties. Sombrero hats tended to overdo the influence but they were very popular and many tourists could not resist returning from their holidays with at least one. Mexican style cotton lawn shirts with ruffle trimmed fronts or gathered peasant blouses and skirts edged with traditional embroideries were more flattering and became established summer styles for several years.

Evening skirts and tops took up the South American look. The tops had wide frilled sleeves but the bodices finished several inches above the waist leaving a bare midriff. The skirts were draped and edged in frills to match the sleeves. Strong colours and bold prints were used for the outfits and Hollywood adapted the style for many colourful musical films. Carmen Miranda, the dynamic singer and dancer who came from Brazil, helped to make midriff styles famous. She was very short and to add height to her outfits she wore enormous turbans or basket-shaped head-dresses decorated with enough fruit to feed a family. As she danced she showed glimpses of very high-heeled gold sandals with deep platform soles.

Although America didn't produce any new silhouettes, they introduced and developed many of their own styles and started new attitudes towards dressing that were adopted in Europe during the following two decades.

Prosperous suburban life became firmly established in America during the 1940s. It was a casual and comfortable way of life, less formal than middle-class life had been in Europe before the war. American homes were well equipped and usually run without domestic help. Many families had two cars and women drove considerable distances to schools, shops and sports centres. Home entertaining was often informal with outdoor barbecue parties in the summer.

American women needed practical clothes for their way of life. Their everyday outfits were based on interchangeable separates – jackets, blouses, knitwear, skirts and trousers. Fussy

In contrast to wartime Europe, America was a fashion Utopia where glamorous and stylish clothes were readily available.

Rita Hayworth was famed for her long red hair which she tossed about provocatively in the film *Gilda*.

Carmen Miranda, the dynamic singer and dancer, helped to make mid-riff styles and enormous turbans famous.

The author aged about 7 — neat short hair and buttoned up school suit.

Little girl's tailored coat and hat still followed the style of the thirties.

hats, formal-looking suits and dresses were kept for trips to the city or for special occasions. It was the beginning of a new more casual approach to following fashion.

Special teenage fashions started in America during the thirties had become more important in the 1940s, and since then teenage clothes have become a permanent part of contemporary fashion. Teenage-girl styles in the forties tended to be either girlishly feminine or casual and boyish. Girlish styles had long loose hair which was pinned up in the front, pushed through a band that was sometimes tied in a bow, or loosely waved and curled from a side parting to the shoulders. Very feminine blouses and skirts were made in blue and white or red and white gingham checks trimmed with broderie anglaise. The blouses had puffed sleeves or wide elasticated necklines that could be pulled down to show bare shoulders. Matching skirts were flared or gathered into wide waistbands. White ankle socks and wedge-heeled sandals completed the outfits. For the boyish style of dressing long hair was taken back into a knot or tied in two side bunches. Long over-sized sweaters called 'sloppy Joes' was a popular teenage craze. They were worn with straightish skirts, trousers or rolled-up blue denim jeans and white socks and gym shoes.

Jeans were still considered rather workmanlike garments. They had originally been worn by 19th-century gold prospectors and cowboys as tough working pants. In the forties jeans were not worn as tightly fitting as in the later decades. Girls wore them for cycling, housework or general lazing around. Girls in sloppy Joe sweaters and jeans were often called 'tom boys'.

American film stars in the forties were as strong an influence on the way many women looked as they had been in the thirties. Because of the war it was harder for women, particularly outside America, to copy the clothes worn in the films, but the looks, hair styles and figures of the stars were a major influence. Veronica Lake became world famous for her long blond hair which was waved downwards covering most of one eye and turned under in a long page-boy style on her shoulders. It was the archetypal Hollywood film star's hair style. During the forties hair styles like it were always called 'Veronica Lake hair-do's'.

Vivacious Rita Hayworth was famed for her long wavy red hair which she tossed about so provocatively in the well known film *Gilda*. Her sex appeal when she danced and sang to 'Put the Blame on Mame' made a lasting impression on many people. Lively girls with long red hair styles were often described as looking like Rita Hayworth.

Lana Turner's curves showing under a tight sweater got her the name of 'The Sweater Girl'. Girls who were similarly endowed and wore tight sweaters were also called 'Sweater Girls'.

Betty Grable was known as 'The Forces' Favourite'. She had remarkably good legs. A famous picture of her in a swimsuit decorated the side of many war planes. Girls with good legs were complimented on their 'Betty Grable' legs.

Between 1942 and 1945 when America had become involved in the war, some restrictions and shortages affected clothing but they were very moderate by European standards of the time. Visitors from Europe were overwhelmed by the selection of smart looking clothes in the American shops.

Although some men found the styles rather brash, American fashions dominated menswear for most of the 1940s. The fashionable silhouette gave men a wedge-shaped line; trilby hats with wide brims topped jackets and coats that hung loosely from heavily padded shoulders. Waist lines were only slightly indicated and trousers were cut wide and straight from the seat to turned up cuffs which broke in a fold on round-toed shoes.

Shirts were loose fitting. Revers, collars and ties were always cut in wide shapes. Ties were sometimes garishly patterned with drawings of pin-up girls or abstract designs that looked like streaks of lightening.

Summer clothes were made in brighter colours. Sky blues and creamy beiges were used for gaberdine town suits. Casual trousers in strong reds, greens and blues were teamed with toning pattern shirts which were often worn outside the trousers.

Resort clothes were even more colourful. Cotton Hawaiian prints in yellow and turquoise or green and orange were used for short-sleeved shirts with matching boxer-style shorts. They were named after the famous Copacabana Beach and were called 'cobana sets'.

Western holidays, staying at ranch-style hotels and seeing the countryside from horseback, became increasingly popular. Many men needed little encouragement to dress up in pseudo-cowboy clothes. After their holidays they started wearing Western clothes for barbecue parties and general weekend wear and manufacturers soon began to produce cowboy-style shirts in bright checks or red or blue satin cotton trimmed with white piping as all-purpose sports shirts.

Shoe styles followed the fashionable broad look and had well rounded toes. There were many more casual slip-on shoes with thick crêpe soles and heels. Some styles had shallow wedge heels similar to the women's shoes. Moccasins in deep reddy-brown leather worn with

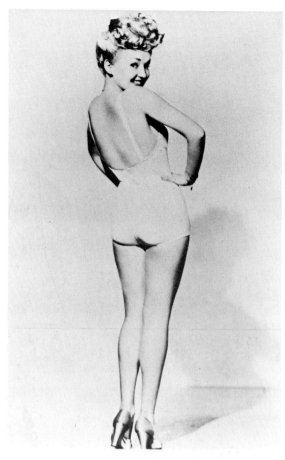

Betty Grable's picture showing her remarkably good legs decorated the side of many war planes.

American GIs buying perfume in Paris soon after the liberation in 1944.

white or yellow socks became a very popular basic style with many younger men. Moccasins with varying shaped toes have remained a standard shoe style up to the present day.

To adapt to the changing type of warfare, uniforms became more functional during the Second World War. The differences in the uniforms worn by all ranks in the British and American Forces were less marked than they had been in the First War. The mechanisation of the Army and the growth and importance of the Air Force made the idea of officers dressing as if they all belonged to cavalry regiments ridiculously out-of-date. Breeches and riding boots were reserved for real cavalry officers to wear for special occasions. Most cavalry officers in the early forties were spending their time sitting in tanks rather than on the backs of horses. Officers still wore tunics and Sam Brown belts but battle dress jackets worn with trousers and shoes or short gaiters and ankle boots were more generally worn.

In Britain, Air Force pilots were admired and hero-worshipped. They were called 'glamour boys' or more unkindly 'Brylcreem boys' although it was their large handlebar moustaches rather than the hair cream that was the fashion feature. The RAF had their own slang – something good was 'wizard' or 'wizard prang'. When they rushed to get into their planes they 'scrambled', and many photographs showed them waiting to 'scramble'. They were shown reading or listening to appropriate popular songs like Vera Lynn's *Bluebirds over the white cliffs of Dover'*. They were wearing combat clothes with flying jackets over non-regulation scarves, flying boots were on and helmets were lying nearby ready to pull on at the last moment.

The American Forces, particularly the ordinary ranks, had smarter uniforms in better quality fabrics than those worn by other Armies. When the 'Yanks' were posted to Britain many girls were impressed by their uniforms, their free spending and the professionalism of their jitterbugging on the dance floor.

An RAF pilot in his flying kit awaiting take-off.

When men were demobilised they were given a civilian outfit. 'Demob suits' were often criticised but many men wore them for several years.

Early post-war swimsuits showed off figures better than ever before.

Short hair was insisted on in the Armed Forces. Some Americans had a short over-all cut leaving the hair on top of the head evenly cropped and brush-like. It was called a 'crew-cut' and it became one of the new styles of the forties. It was not always very flattering but some men liked it and found it easy to manage and kept their 'crew cuts' in civilian life.

When men were demobilised at the end of the war they were given a civilian outfit, a suit, shirt and tie, shoes and a raincoat. 'Demob suits' were often criticised for being in poor quality fabrics and lacking in style but many men were glad to get them. Some ex-servicemen were too young to have had adult clothes before the war; others had changed shape or their clothes had been lost in air-raids. Despite all the detrimental remarks many men wore their demob suits for many years.

In the post-war austerity years money was often made by selling scarce items at inflated prices. Some men found it more profitable to deal on the Black Market than to take conventional jobs. They were called 'spivs'. Spivs had their own flashy way of dressing. They wore wide brimmed American style trilby hats tilted forward over one eye, overlarge top coats and suits with exaggeratedly padded shoulders and round-toed crêpe soled suede shoes. Any man who dressed in a slightly over slick way was often called 'spivy'.

In 1944, with the end of the European war almost in sight, English *Vogue* published an interview with Hardy Amies the well known designer, and James Laver the fashion historian, on how they saw fashion developing in the post-war years. Hardy Amies thought women would be ready for figure-fitting lines with full skirts and a revival of Victorian and Edwardian femininity. James Laver pointed out that after major wars and revolutions women tended to cut their hair short and wear scimpy clothes with the waistline in the wrong place. They were both proved to be right but the revival of femininity came first.

As early as the spring of 1945 the French couture designers, anxious to re-establish Paris as the creative centre of fashion, began to promote a rounder, more feminine silhouette, less padded at the shoulder, small waisted and with slightly longer skirts. The Paris collections were given plenty of publicity. Women read about them with interest but they were not quite ready to take them up. The circumstances in 1945 were completely different from 1919. In Europe it was not possible to follow new fashion silhouettes – most commodities were in short supply. Rationing and currency restrictions were strictly enforced, particularly in Britain. There were far fewer rich individual customers and the old style of social life which required many different types of fashionable outfits was not revived on the pre-war scale. The couture houses had to find new markets for their designs and convince women that seasonal fashion changes were important. American garment manufacturers became the most important customers. Although America had developed many of its own fashions and had managed quite well without European styles, they had an ever-growing clothing industry which needed a constant supply of new ideas. Wholesale manufacturers used the Paris collections as a source of new trends. They paid a considerable entrance fee to see each collection and sometimes bought models and patterns to copy and adapt for the American market.

Between 1945 and 1947 the Paris designers softened and feminised their lines a little more each season. Day clothes were less boxy looking. Cocktail and evening outfits were more dressy and were slightly influenced by the fashions of the early 1910s with hip drapery and peg top effects.

Early post-war suit with square shoulders, long jacket and short boxy skirt.

By 1947 the newer looking styles were beginning to appear even in austere Britain. The feminine silhouette was gradually easing its way in. A rather controlled pace for post-war fashion changes appeared to be set.

In the spring of 1947 Dior launched his now legendary 'New Look'. All the tentative new fashion lines were exaggerated beyond most people's wildest dreams and Christian Dior earned himself a prominent place in the history of fashion.

The New Look changed fashion from head to toe. Hair was brushed smoothly into a chignon on the crown of the·head or swept and rolled to one side. Hats were smaller, softer shapes, usually pillboxes or berets worn on the back or the side of the head and lightly trimmed with veiling or a group of feathers. Shoulders were very sloped and emphasised the downward line. They were sometimes cut full under the armhole in a dolman shape. Sleeves were often three-quarter length and worn with long slightly ruched gloves which gave the lower arms a very delicate feminine look. Breasts were more exaggerated than they had been since the early 1900s, but unlike the full lowish busts of the Edwardian matrons, the New Look pushed the breasts up and outwards. The rib cage was fitted like a second skin and waists were pulled in to sizes that might have daunted the Victorians. Hips were highlighted with short fluted jackets. Skirts were either skin-tight hobbles or very full swirling pleats or flares; sometimes as much as 25 yards of material was used in one skirt. Day lengths varied from the bottom of the calf to just above the ankle. Stockings were a smoky-grey beige colour and shoes were plain high-heeled court shoes or finely strapped round the ankles.

To achieve the New Look shape, constructing undergarments were needed, special bras to lift the breasts, boned corselettes called 'waspies' to minimise the waists, petticoats, and for some dresses hip and stomach pads to hold the skirt fullness out in a pannier effect.

Fashion had taken up where it left off in 1939 with a neo-Victorian revival but the new styles were far more extreme. The New Look in its most exaggerated form was rarely worn but its influence was far-reaching and lasted for many years and it firmly re-established Paris as the creative fashion centre of the world.

It is difficult to overstate the impact of the New Look. It would have been considered an extravagant fashion in affluent times. The early months of 1947 had produced some of the coldest weather ever known, fuel was desperately short, and in parts of Europe people died from the cold. Power cuts, rationing and shortages had never been as severe. Dior models dressed in his most extreme styles, waiting to be photographed by a food market, had their clothes torn by infuriated women who had been trying to find enough food for their families.

Paris fashions in 1946. Hats were worn on the back of the head, shoulders less square, waists smaller and slightly longer skirts.

Dior's 'New Look' in 1947. Skin-tight bodices, nipped-in waists and long full skirts.

A short softer jacket and long full skirt was to follow the 'New Look' one year later.

In Britain the Government seriously considered prohibiting the production of the new styles and people were appealed to publicly to boycott the new fashions for patriotic reasons. Women dressed in unflattering caricatures of the New Look paraded with placards proclaiming 'Don't be daft, Mr Dior'.

Even in prosperous America where women had followed early post-war fashions, some women campaigned for 'Just Below the Knee Clubs', asking for a commitment from women not to wear the longer skirts.

Despite the outcries and the hostile reactions, more and more women hankered for the new styles. It was a natural reaction from the war and austerity. Women wanted to wear feminine dresses with yards of material swishing around their legs. It was like showing ragged Cinderella her ball dress. Within six months the new fashions had taken on in America and in Britain women were trying to lengthen their skirts and if possible make their clothes more up-to-date, rather like they had done in 1930, but in 1947 it was a shortage of material rather than the lack of money that was the main problem.

There were several popular ways of up-dating dresses. A small amount of a contrast fabric such as velvet or silk was made into a corselette band and inserted between the bottom of the rib cage and the top of the hips. In theory the skirt hemline should have been dropped several inches; in practice, women who were even slightly plump round the waist, stomach or hips, gathered the inset band into folds round the middle and the hemline length was hardly altered. Bands of fabric stitched round the bottom of the skirt was an easier and more effective way of ensuring a definite drop in length.

Early in 1948 a friend of my mother's returned from America with one of the first New
Look suits we had seen; it was in pale blue corded silk with a short jacket nipped in at the
waist and flared over the hips in two back dipping flounces. The skirt was lower calf length
and very flared with extra fullness in the back to complement the back interest of the jacket.
The outfit caused a local sensation. People turned round in the street, stared from buses, cars
even stopped so that women could get out and have a closer look at the suit and find out
where it came from.

During 1948 fashionable women in Europe thoroughly enjoyed wearing their first New
Look clothes. They were modified versions of the Dior designs but they were quite different

Women enjoying
the 'New Look' in 1948,
London's bomb damaged
streets in the background.

A wholesale adaptation of one of the lines that
followed the 'New Look' – shorter skirt and loose
back panel.

*"By 'New Look' I take it you mean what we now
consider 'Old Look', but not the 'Old Look' which
preceded the 'New Look'."*

from the styles of even one year earlier. Comparing illustrations of medium-priced dresses and
suits for spring 1947 and spring 1948, the completely changed silhouette would usually have
taken four or five years even in the fashion conscious twenties and thirties.

After the war, evening dresses were not as important or as widely worn as they had been in
the thirties. Upper-class women did not automatically change into evening dress for dinner
and the theatre. Evening dresses became reserved for special occasions. The post-war styles
were quite formal and regal looking with tightly-fitting bodices and full crinoline-style skirts.
The feminine lines of the New Look with full lower calf-length hemlines were very suitable
for informal evening wear. Day lengths, or as they were often called, 'ballet length' dresses,
quickly became an established style for attending restaurants, theatres, parties and informal
dances.

Rationing and shortages had affected children's clothes as much as adults'. Private schools
in Britain had to relax their insistence on specified school uniforms. Older boys and girls
sometimes took advantage of the relaxed rules and went to school in quite modern grown-up

styles. If their clothes were disapproved of they usually claimed the conventional school outfits were unavailable.

Some girls still had their hair short and neat looking, similar to the styles introduced in the twenties and also worn in the thirties but many girls had long hair, and like the women of the 1940s, arranged it in various, albeit less contrived, styles. Girls put their hair in plaits, or the hair was parted at the side or in the middle and held by hairpins or slides and neatly waved or curled onto the shoulders.

The more extreme figure-fitting lines of the New Look could not be worn by girls with adolescent figures but girls in their early teens wanted to be included in the new fashions. Skirts and party dresses were cut fuller with gathers or flares and longer calf-length hemlines. After school hours girls anxious to look modern and more grown-up changed from their short gym slips and school skirts into the new longer styles.

The new ideas in boys' clothes were American, casual T-shirts and brightly patterned or checked sports shirts became established basic garments. Military style battle-dress jackets and zip-fronted jerkins were adapted for boys. They were practical styles and boys used to seeing their fathers in uniform liked the military influence for their own clothes.

The young post-war generation in their late teens and early twenties followed fashion in a more casual and careless way than the early generation. The effects of the war had cut across the class divisions and although class distinction through dress remained, it was far less noticeable amongst the young.

After the war young men rarely wore hats. More attention was paid to their hair styles. Hair was still short and conventional looking by later standards but a wider variety of styles was becoming acceptable. Hair was always cut short at the back but there were several ways of wearing the top hair. It could be shorn in the 'crew cut' or left long on top and allowed to fall into ungreased waves or curls. Hair cream was still widely used but even the more set looking styles were arranged in rather high waves. The flattened hair of the early decades was considered out-of-date.

Many young men, especially students, wore parts of their old service kit or bought them from Army surplus stores. Duffle coats and sheepskin-lined flying jackets were very popular.

Apart from public transport, cycling was the way most girls travelled around their districts. Although they liked the new long skirts they were impractical on bicycles and girls started to wear American style trousers called 'pedal pushers'. They were rolled up or cut off at the calf. In the winter, to give an American college girl look, 'pedal pushers' were worn with big pullovers, mannish jackets or duffle coats, brightly coloured men's socks, and flat or wedge-heeled shoes. Shoulder revealing blouses or sun tops were worn with summer 'pedal pushers'. Trousers were an established casual wear fashion but they were still not worn as an everyday town style. They were associated with the war years and factory workers and looked masculine amongst the more feminine styles of the late forties.

For everyday wear most girls wore tops and skirts. Blouses and knitwear had natural or sloping shoulders. Sweaters were sometimes cut with deep raglan or dolman sleeves. Skirts were either very full or very narrow. In-between widths with a few pleats or little gathering were considered pre-New Look and dowdily old-fashioned. The most popular full skirt was the dirndl style. It was a wide piece of material gathered into a broad waist band. It was an easy style for the home dressmaker and was the first garment many girls learnt to make.

Barbara Goalen, England's famous
post-war model, with the new short
hairstyle and full-skirted ball dress.

All-black outfits, black sweater, skirt and shoes, were thought to be sophisticated and
grown-up looking. Girls often wore them at parties when they listened and danced to
traditional jazz which was enjoying a successful revival. Many of the younger generation
found jazz more exciting than the commercialised swing music of the time.

Clothing manufacturers were beginning to realise the potential of the young market. They
started to produce young-looking inexpensive dresses, particularly for the summer. One of the
best known names in Britain was Horrockses. Their cotton dresses were very popular and
stores throughout the country gave them special window displays. Strapless cotton printed
dresses with matching bolero jackets was one of the most successful styles. Girls wore them for
many different occasions. They were worn with the boleros on as a summer town outfit and
some girls went to work in offices wearing them. Without the jacket the dress could be worn
on the beach or for sunbathing in the garden, and for parties and dances they were easily
dressed up with a little jewellery and a pair of high-heeled shoes.

Swimwear was very popular with the young generation. Well fitting one- and two-piece
suits helped to show off young figures better than ever before. American styles and fit were
the most progressive. They were made in elasticated fabrics with a satin finish and were either
in strong plain colours or bright prints. Design features like most of the fashions of the time,

emphasised the bust and the waist. Styles were draped over the bust or ruched down the centre front. The two-piece suits were becoming noticeably smaller and the first bikini sets appeared. They were called after the atomic bomb tested at Bikini Atoll and were thought to be the ultimate in daring exposure. Most women felt they were far too revealing and were happy to leave them to be worn by advanced Californian women or publicity-seeking starlets on the beaches at Cannes during the Film Festival.

Once the Paris designers had proved they could change the basic silhouette completely, they were anxious to keep the fashion lead. The New Look was followed by a series of newer looks. The 'Tube Look' was launched for Autumn 1948. Hair was shorter and neater. Hats revived the head-fitting cloche shapes, but unlike the 1920s helmet cloches the newer styles were softer and showed more of the face and the hair. Shoulders were still sloping and waists tightly nipped in but bodices and skirts moulded the curves of the figure rather than exaggerating them. Skirts were narrower and slightly shorter. The following season the 'Tube Look' had developed into the 'Maypole Line' with loose flying panels over very tight skirts.

Two new silhouettes with mid-calf length hemlines were shown in the Paris collections for Autumn 1949, the 'geometric line' and the 'bloused look'. The geometric line featured sharp angular designs on the basic tube shape of the previous year. Collars and revers were cut into upward or downward points. Skirts were back wrapped into uncomfortable angled folds or draped across the front and stiffened into a triangular shape on one hip. Bodices with the bloused look were cut like loose shirts with over-wide dropped shoulder lines, tightly belted so that they bloused above and below the waistline. Skirt shapes worn with the bloused tops were very narrow and tapered.

The press gave plenty of publicity to the succession of 'looks' and 'lines' but women couldn't keep up with the changes and many felt bewildered by all the fashion news.

Punch showed a drawing of a rather timid woman in a fashion department talking to a superior looking saleslady who was patronisingly testing the woman's fashion knowledge by saying, 'I presume by the New Look Madam means what we now consider the Old Look, but not of course the Old Look that preceded the New Look'.

Few women wore the more extreme Paris lines of the late forties. The seasonal fashion changes were adapted as style variations rather than important new lines. The basic figure-emphasising silhouette with full or narrow calf-length skirts was firmly established.

Other areas of fashion, hair styles, make-up and accessories, changed to suit the established silhouette.

During 1948 and 1949 James Laver's prediction that post-war women would cut their hair short proved correct. The long complicated hair styles that had been worn since the thirties looked heavy and fussy with the feminine sloping shoulders. Short hair styles were introduced. The press scared some women by talking about a return to the 'twenties crop'. In fact, the hair styles of the late forties were softer and easier to wear. They were parted at the side or cut in a soft fringe and lightly waved or curled at the sides and back, or the hair was turned under in the 'cap cut' which was a short version of the popular page-boy style. Some women who were used to their long film-star styles were nervous in case short hair was less flattering and made them look older. Once they had it cut many women were pleasantly surprised to find the short styles looked younger and fresher.

The most extreme cut in 1949 was the 'urchin cut' — very short hair was brushed forward

One of the short haircuts of the late forties. Ropes of pearls and long gloves were fashionable accessories.

over the ears and forehead in irregular rather wispy points. It was a high fashion style, very popular with leading model girls like the well known English model Barbara Goalen. Although it was not an easy style for some women to wear, women with small features and sensitive faces looked rather wistful and appealing with their urchin cuts.

With shorter hair, make-up emphasis changed. Eyes were highlighted, the heavy red mouth was no longer the focal point. Eyebrows were thickly pencilled, eyes were outlined and the corners were slightly elongated and slanted upwards. It was called the 'doe eyed' look. Eyes became the most emphasised part of make-up for the next ten years.

Although women wore hats less frequently, they were still considered an important part of fashion. During the late forties most hats were neat head-fitting shapes, moderately trimmed with bunches of ribbons, flowers or feathers. One or two long, dangerously-angled feathers sticking up several inches above the hat were attached to fashion conscious autumn hats. Large summer hats made in straw or felt were worn on top of the head. They looked quite dramatic with their broader-than-shoulder-width brims topping figure-fitting dresses and suits.

Fashionable accessories were more refined and elegant looking to complement the feminine lines of the clothes.

Elbow-length gloves in fine kid or soft suede were worn with dressy day and cocktail outfits. Gloves were sometimes pulled over narrow full-length sleeves but many dresses and some suits had three-quarter length sleeves specially designed to show long gloves.

Fashionable jewellery changed. Short hair and sloping shoulders made necks look long and slender. Dangling earrings were revived for evening wear and long ropes of pearls with matching pearl stud earrings became extremely popular, particularly with all-black outfits.

Shoulder bags were still worn with casual clothes but with dressy day outfits smaller bags were carried in the hand or hung from the wrists. Many of the designs were soft and pouch shaped. They were sometimes gathered across the top and clasp fastenings were small and neat.

Shoes were more delicate. Plain high-heeled court shoes in black leather or suede became the predominant shoe style. The shape was unexaggerated, heels were not noticeably thin or thick, toes were generally rounded. The classic cut-out curve at the front of the court shoe was usually cut in a V-shape. Open toed, sling-back shoes with high heels, platform soles and ankle straps were still popular, especially with cocktail and short evening dresses but they were more elegantly shaped. Sports and casual shoes were also less clumsy looking. Wedge heels were still worn but they were shallower wedged, often joined to flat rather than platform soles.

Accessories in 1949 began to give clothes a slight 1920s look. Head-fitting hats, short hair styles, long earrings and slim plain court shoes were all reminiscent of that period.

There was a nostalgia for the earlier post-war period, particularly amongst the young generation born in the early thirties. They read books written in the twenties, their parents taught them the Charleston and girls, enjoyed dressing up as flappers with headbands and long cigarette holders for 1920s parties.

The fashion press began to talk about a return to the 'Roaring twenties' with straight lines and short skirts. Although fashion had a 'twenties look', clothes were very fitted and moulded the figure. The silhouette at the end of the forties was nearer to the 1900 shape than at any time before or since.

Straight lines and short skirts became fashionable in the second half of the following decade as everyday styles for the mass market. They were a later post-war fashion but they were brought about by the social changes caused by the Second World War, and James Laver's theory that scimpy clothes follow wars and revolutions proved to be right.

At the end of the forties the clothing industry all over the world was expanding. Women in many countries still had to put up with shortages and lack of selection but things were improving. Clothes rationing ended in Britain in 1949, and fashionable women were increasing in most European cities.

The American clothing industry led the world with their mass produced clothes. The latest Dior designs were adapted for the American market and were in the chain stores within a few weeks of their first showing in Paris. More women had the opportunity to be dressed in the latest fashions than ever before.

Despite the sobering atmosphere of the 'Cold War', America and many parts of the world had a brighter decade ahead of them. New fashions for the masses and the 'Affluent Society' were on the way.

The 1950s

John Cavanagh's fashionable coats were formal and ladylike with gloves and hats.

1950 suit, tightly fitted body and waist, stiffened over the hips, narrow slit skirt.

At the beginning of the 1950s few people realised that the world was entering a more prosperous era. Living standards for many people improved steadily as the decade progressed. Post-war reconstruction was followed by the start of a prolonged period of expansion and development in trade and industry. The comparatively prosperous times benefited a far greater proportion of the population than earlier industrial booms. More people had money for consumer goods and there was an ever-growing market for fashion conscious clothes at all price levels.

Clothes in the early fifties were less formal than they had been before the war but women still followed fashion in a conformist way. Clothes were categorised, pre-war ideas on appropriate styles for different occasions were revived in a modified form and women accepted the lead given by the top designers.

The Paris designers unquestionably set the new fashions, their original ideas were adapted by the wholesale clothing manufacturers and the majority of clothing conscious women wore simplified versions of the Paris styles within a season or two of their first introduction.

Dior and Balenciaga were the supreme dictators, they set a high standard of taste and style in fashionable dressing. In the early part of the decade, cut, fit and line were the important features of their designs. Dior became famous for his ultra-feminine styles with accentuated figures and extravagantly full skirts. By 1950 his designs were less frivolous, they still emphasised womanly curves with large breasts and small waists but the design details of the garments were simpler and he used material less lavishly. The combination of cut and fit with simpler styling looked elegant and lady-like on tall women with well-shaped figures and a good sense of poise and deportment.

Clothes were very constructed. Shirley Worthington in shaped bra is about to put on a dress with its own boned underbodice.

The couture designers set the fashions – Dior's ball dress shown to an attentive audience.

Balenciaga was Spanish by birth, he left Spain during the civil war and after a brief spell in London settled in Paris where he opened his couture house in the late thirties. He quickly became a well respected designer known for his advanced ideas. Dior's great successes in 1947 and 48 had temporarily eclipsed Balenciaga's fame, however by the early fifties he was firmly established as a designer of equal authority.

In 1951 Balenciaga began to move away from clothes that were tightly shaped to the figure and develop a new approach to fit. His new suit and coat designs only indicated the bust and waist in the front, the back hung straight or curved slightly outwards from the shoulder blades – it was called the 'semi-fitted look'.

Balenciaga like Chanel believed in understated design details and easy fit, but unlike Chanel's soft fluid lines, Balenciaga's clothes were constructed and sculptured looking. They had harder flatter lines, interlining was used to give collars and the body of the garment a definite shape. Some of his jackets and coats were cut rather like a high fastening military tunic with a shaped collar around the neck instead of the conventional collar and revers. The collars were set about one inch away from the neck to give a stand away effect and Balenciaga became well known for this new style in the early fifties.

The semi-fitted line was considered a very high fashion style at first, but within a few seasons other designers were showing the new easy fit as an alternative shape. The idea that differing types of cut and fit could be equally fashionable was a welcome new development. Even though designers clearly defined their fashion lines and the press reported them rather reverently, women began to follow fashion in a more relaxed way. They felt somewhat unsure about sudden fashion changes in case a single dominant line outdated their entire wardrobes as the New Look had done in the late forties. The press tended to play on this by over-emphasising each season's fashion changes, especially any alteration in skirt lengths. Despite the wide variety in the length of women's legs, hemlines were always given as so many inches from the ground. In 1951 *Vogue* noted the length as between 13 and 15 in. For autumn 1952 skirts were reported as definitely longer, down to 11¼ in from the floor. In July 1953 the news that Dior had raised some of his hemlines as high as 16 or 17 in made the front page of many national newspapers.

Very few women bothered to adjust their skirts a couple of inches up or down, hemlines for day clothes were generally worn to about the middle of the calf for the first half of the decade, cocktail and informal evening dresses were usually slightly longer.

Hair was always neat looking, both short or long styles were fashionable. Short uncontrived hairstyles were based on skilful cutting and shaping, hard set waves and pinned curls were considered old-fashioned and provincial looking. New hairdressers with a good reputation for modern cutting quickly developed a strong following with the younger generation. Hair was cut to follow the natural shape of the head, it was parted at the side or in the centre, sometimes with a straight or slightly waved fringe and then gradually shaped back to turn under at the nape of the neck; or the hair was brushed straight back without a parting and layered into a ducks-tail effect.

As an alternative to straightish styles, hair was sometimes permed into the 'bubble cut' with short all over curls. Mary Martin the star in the successful American musical *South Pacific* helped popularise the short curly cut, she shampooed her hair during every stage performance as part of the routine of her well known song 'I'm going to wash that man right out of my hair'.

Slightly shorter, neater versions of the long filmstar styles so popular in the late thirties and forties were still worn by some women, but the more elegant long hair styles were smoothly brushed in a knot on the crown of the head or at the nape of the neck. Hair worn like this suited the lines of the fashionable clothes with their constructed shapes and stand away necklines.

Girls in their teens and early twenties often tied long hair back with a ribbon so that it sprung out from the crown of the head to fall in a loose pony-tail. A swinging pony-tail became very characteristic of the fifties.

The decline in wearing hats continued but they were still a part of the fashion picture. Newspapers and magazines carried regular features just on hats. Stores had quite extensive hat departments and an allocated permanent window space for displaying them. Most towns and suburbs had several hat shops – these were successful small businesses where the proprietor bought with the social life of his clients in mind. Regular customers, particularly middle-aged and older women, would buy new styles each season. Many women still felt a hat should be worn to complete her outfit even if she was only visiting her local town or city.

Hat designs tended to complement outfits rather than form the focal point. Design details were quiet but styles and shapes varied. The head-fitting cloche reintroduced in the late forties carried on into the early fifties. The newer more sophisticated styles covered all the side and back hair, they were often made in jersey and draped into neat turbans. It was the ideal style for showing off pearl, gold or rhinestone ear-rings; stud-shaped ear-rings were popular throughout the fifties with day clothes, sportswear and evening dresses.

Long hair was brushed smoothly back and pinned into a 'french pleat'.

The high fashion hat style of the early fifties was the small pill box worn straight across the forehead.

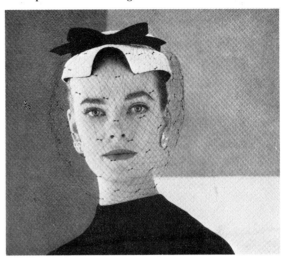

Since it was not possible to wear a blouse under the tightly-fitting suits, necklines were filled in with scarves.

The press were very hemline conscious and changes in
length were often given front page coverage.

In the early fifties Balanciaga began to move away
from tight shaping and develop his 'semi-fitted look'.

Tailored clothes were still the most important garments. London's 'top twelve' designers showed elegant conservative styles in 1954.

New hat shapes were all designed to be worn straight on top of the head and boaters, flat pancake berets and coolie hats were all popular. Coolie hats varied in size from shallow saucer shapes just big enough to span the head, to deeper fitting summer straw hats with should-wide brims. The high-fashion hat style was the small pill box worn straight across the forehead, heavy make-up outlined the eyes and eyebrows and no front or side hair showed. It was a severely elegant style that looked its best on women with good features and long slender necks.

Tailored clothes were the important basic garments in most womens wardrobes – they were expensive items to buy and had to be carefully chosen so that they could be worn for several seasons. Fashion magazines offered regular advice on the selection of styles, often illustrating the versatility of a certain garment by photographing it several times with different accessories.

Suit jackets were fitted or semi-fitted (in the first half of the decade the fitted line was still the most popular) and were sharply darted and seamed into the waist. A tape was sometimes stitched around the waist under the lining to pull the waistline in even more firmly. It was often impossible to wear a blouse under the closely-shaped jackets, and bare necklines and fronts were filled in with rows of pearls or a scarf. Jacket lengths were usually quite short, finishing just below the hip bones. Matching skirts were nearly always narrow, gripping the hips and tapering in at the hem; to allow for ease of movement there was usually a slit or a short pleat at the side or in the back. Skirts were made to look skin tight in fashion photographs, showing every curve of the hips and legs. The models posed for pictures with one leg in front of the other and the back of the skirt was pinned or pegged in giving an impossibly small circumference around the hem.

Many tweed topcoats were tightly shaped to the figure.

Topcoats were very fitted following the same body shape as the suit jackets, or loose and full. The in between semi-fitted or straight coats were occasionally worn but became more generally popular later in the decade. Body-shaped coats with longish flared skirts were quite feminine and flattering but the variety of clothes that could be worn under them was limited. Loose flowing coats were roomy enough to go over every jacket shape and dresses with very full skirts, although they were rather cumbersome, unless carefully arranged, and tended to get caught in car doors, knock ornaments off low tables and sweep over stairs.

Fabrics and colours for tailored clothes were quiet and understated. Materials were usually made from natural fibres and were of a higher quality than many of the fabrics used in later decades. Most synthetic fibres were still in the development stage, although rayon which had been available since before the war was sometimes used for summer suits and dresses.

Neutral colours were the most popular shades for woollens and tweeds; greys, beiges, and black, white and grey mixtures were used for coats, suits and autumn dresses. Black or grey flannel and gaberdine were the most popular colours and fabrics for sharply tailored suits. Topcoats in heavy black face cloth were widely worn as all purpose city coats.

Although easy fit was gradually gaining favour for suits, dress bodices were always closely shaped to the figure and nipped into the waist with a wide elasticated belt or a narrow leather or fabric belt pulled into the last bearable notch. Skirts were very narrow and tapered like the suit skirt or very full and flared. Narrow skirts were more popular for autumn dresses, the heavy woollen fabrics suited the clinging lines.

Summer dresses usually had very wide skirts gathered into the waistline or cut in a circle to give equally flared fullness all around the skirt. During the summer, neatly dressed young

'Sheath' dresses showed every curve
of the figure. Long gloves were often
worn with sleeveless dresses.

Constructed undergarments were needed to achieve
the demanding lines of the 'sheath' dress.

women with tidy hair styles, the occasional small hat, short white gloves and feminine looking cotton print dresses with full bouncy skirts filled city streets.

In 1952 and 53 Dior promoted unbelted 'sheath dresses', which moulded the body from the shoulder to the narrow hemline and showed the slightest bulge. Although it was a line that needed a flawless figure, sheath dresses became a surprisingly popular style for several years.

Evening dresses were very constructed to achieve the Victorian-type silhouette, with small tight tops and full crinoline-style skirts. The tops were strapless or had daringly low plunging neck lines, and were usually mounted on a boned underbodice which was sometimes fitted to a customer's shape. Very full skirts were worn over several petticoats, the skirt and petticoat sometimes being joined together. Dresses were so heavily constructed that they could stand rigid on the floor waiting for the wearer to step in.

Dresses were made in a combination of fabrics, the bodice in draped satin and the big skirt in layers of tulle, sometimes in different but complementary colours like pinks with grey or soft blues and greens, giving a shaded effect. Couturiers and dressmakers were particularly good at achieving attractive and unusual colour combinations. Paper taffeta in white, pale ice-pink or sophisticated black was very popular for ball dresses with rustling skirts. A small party in evening dress, with two or three women in their voluminous skirts, managed to fill the comparatively large cars of the early fifties with yards of uncontrollable material.

Evening dresses usually had their own built-in shape, but to achieve the fashionable figure for day dresses uncomfortable looking undergarments were needed. Bras enlarged the size of the breasts and pushed them up and outwards. Large breasts were a very much admired part of a woman's sex appeal, particularly in America. If a woman felt she was too small, padded or blown up 'falsies' were worn and an unexpectedly deflated or slipped falsie was a great embarrassment! Waists were pulled in with an elasticated or lightly boned 'waspie', suspender belts helped to flatten the stomach and hips, and because tights had yet to be introduced for everyday wear flesh coloured nylon stockings were clipped onto the bottom of the belt. All-in-one figure shaping garments combining bra, waspie and suspender belt were sometimes worn to give a smooth unbroken line, particularly under sheath dresses. Many women did not go in for such elaborate underwear, but bras, suspender belts and stockings were usually worn.

The couture houses were still the most exclusive places for women to buy their clothes; figure-fitting lines and constructed shapes helped the couturiers hold on to their exclusivity. Their expert tailors, fitters and the standard of make in their workrooms could not be achieved in mass produced clothing. A couture design fitted to an individual figure was easily recognisable, however, exclusiveness in fashion lines and style details had gone and wholsesale manufacturers copied any fashion with potential appeal for the mass market.

The British Marks and Spencer stores gained a good reputation for style, cut and quality; their clothes could be afforded by most. Marks and Spencer jersey dresses were particularly successful with women of all ages and classes. Wealthy women wearing their Marks and Spencer jersey dresses would attend fittings at couture houses boasting of the value and chic of their 'finds'. It started many designers thinking seriously about the scope in designing for a wider market.

During the first half of the 1950s fashion reflected a mood of moderate conservatism and nostalgia for a more settled era, the fashionable ideal was once again the mature elegant woman. High fashion models looked well bred, slightly aloof and rather older than their

Ball dresses like this Hardy Amies design shown in 1954 had layers of material to form the crinoline skirts.

years. Photographic modelling was a fashionable career, top models often becoming well known personalities frequently written about by the gossip columnists. France's Battina, America's Susie Parker and Britain's Barbara Goalan and Fiona Campbell-Walter were some of the best known names; they led glamourous lives and some married wealthy influential men.

Women had reverted to figure constraining clothes and men revived the 'Edwardian Look'. Brash American styles of the forties were no longer admired in Europe. England lead the return to more dandified men's fashions. Suits were precisely tailored, jackets were cut with high fastening revers and a line that shaped the figure from under the arms to the waist where it flared out over the hips with side or centre back vents like a riding jacket. Trousers fitted more closely around the hips and tapered down the legs to narrow bottoms. Higher fastening shoes or ankle-covering chukka boots in suede or polished leather helped to give a long elegant line.

Women wore very full skirts using yards of material.

Dresses with a couture fit like this Dior design were easily recognisable.
Stoles were worn with day and evening dresses.

Bust emphasis was nearly always a feature of evening dresses in the early and mid-fifties.

Fancy waistcoats in contrasting colours and fabrics were worn with the new style suits and jackets. Silk waistcosts in light grey, wine, or a deep blue were sometimes worn with dark city suits and although hats were generally worn less frequently a bowler with a curled brim and a rolled umbrella hooked over the arm completed the revived English gentleman style of the 1900s.

Horsey-looking waistcoats in small yellow and beige checks, plain coloured corduroys or bright red or yellow cavalry twill were often worn with tweed suits and sports jackets. Soft felt hats with turned up brims or flat-looking caps with the brims stitched to the crown gave weekend and country clothes an equestrian look. There was a more definite division between fashionable town and country clothes after the casual approach to dress during the early post-war austerity years.

Overcoats followed the Edwardian style – they were closer fitting and shortened to just above the knee to show off the new narrow trouser line. Dressy town coats were usually in smooth fabrics and dark colours, fashion-conscious styles had darker toning velvet collars. Straight camel topcoats with rows of stitching near the hem were a more versatile style, they could be worn equally well with town and country clothes. Double-breasted coats like elegant officers' greatcoats with epaulettes and leather football buttons were made in wool twill or heavy coatings.

Long belted riding macs in cream rubberised cotton also promoted the military look, many young men wore them as all-purpose raincoats. Men in their early twenties had grown used, as children, to seeing their fathers in uniform, war films in the forties always glamorised daring airforce pilots and soldiers, and at 18 young men were conscripted into the armed

For Men Who *Know* Good Clothes

England lead the return to more dandified men's fashions with the 'Edwardian look'. Left: A conventional suit brought up-to-date with a check waistcoat.

forces to do two years military service. The fashionable ideal for men in England amongst the middle and upper classes appeared to evolve into the elegant young officer in civilian dress.

Severe military-looking hairstyles however were not liked by the younger generations who were wearing their hair slightly longer. The short back and sides cut became the older generation's style, or the dreaded cut recruits were subject to at the beginning of their national service. Young men had their hair trimmed rather than cut. The top hair was left long and the weight made it flop forwards, sideboards were longer but still quite moderate by later standards. Greased hair continued to be popular for the more obviously arranged styles but a lot of men thought they looked overdone and too slick.

Mens clothes became far more fashion conscious during the second half of the 20th century. In the fifties younger men welcomed the idea of a more extrovert way of dressing but they were rather timid about going too far with new styles. Only a small minority wore the extreme Edwardian fashions. Simplified versions were adapted for a wider market and the modified new cut in jackets and overcoats became the basic younger man's styles of the time. Shaped double-breasted blazers worn with tapered beige cavalry twill trousers was a very popular uncontroversial style of dressing. To add a touch of individuality, army or club badges were embroidered on the blazer's breast pocket.

The more fashion conscious form of dressing was not only confined to the upper and middle classes. Young working-class men benefited from full employment and the growing prosperity of the fifties, they had more money to spend on clothes and did not want to look like Edwardian gentlemen, but they liked some of the jackets and trouser styles and adapted

James Dean's hairstyle, T-shirt, casual jacket and jeans could easily have been worn 25 years later.

Elvis Presley's appearances in 1956 presented an overtly sexy image, quite new in pop singers.

'Ton-up kids' in leather gear represented an outlet for young aggression.

Although rather homely looking by later standards, ski clothes were becoming more colourful and practical.

them to form their own fashions. They exaggerated the jackets into longer, looser shapes and wore them with a very thin 'slim jim' or bootlace tie. Trousers fitted the legs tightly, 'drain pipes' or 'drains' finished just above the ankle and showed plenty of brightly-coloured socks. With the short trousers, shoes appearing prominently were chunky looking black or navy lace-ups with thick crepe soles.

To complete outfits special attention was paid to hairstyles which were inspired by some of the American filmstars. Hair was heavily greased and brushed into a high forward set wave, sideboards were quite long and the hair was swept back behind the ears into a point at the back of the head. This was called a 'Tony Curtis' after the young star who had worn the style in his early films. Boys dressed in their new fashions were known as 'Teddy boys' or 'Teds'.

Some of the younger generations in Europe and America bought motorbikes and special black leather trousers, jackets and boots – it became one of the later 20th-century cults. Gangs of boys tearing around on bikes with girlfriends riding pillion dressed in sinister looking leather gear seems to have been an outlet for aggression; in England racing down an open road was doing a 'ton' and the riders 'ton-up kids'. This was the beginning of a new era when the working-class set their own fashion rather than following the upper-class lead in a modest form. The new trend developed strongly during the following decades.

Active sportswear carried on with the functional approach to styling developed in the thirties. The longer skirt lengths in day clothes did not affect tennis dresses which remained well above the knee, but the dresses were more figure shaping and girlish petticoats worn

The spring 1957 dresses were getting simpler and shorter.

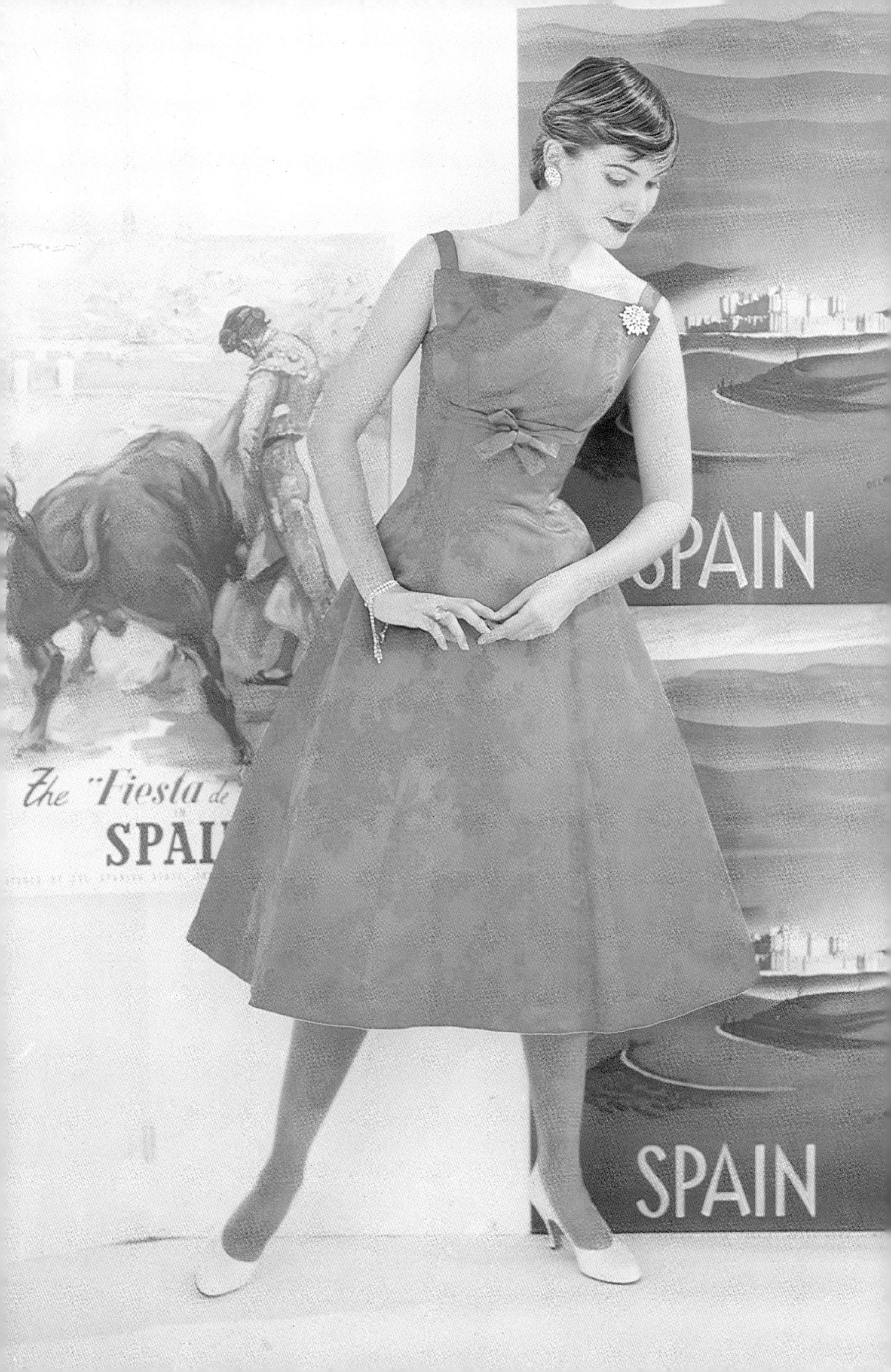
The "Fiesta de
SPAI
SPAIN
SPAIN

under some of them showed with the active movements of the game. Ski clothes became more style conscious, hooded parkas in proofed fabrics were made in bright colours and strong checks, trousers were narrower, and elasticated materials began to be used. Although rather homely by later standards, ski-wear was becoming brighter and more modern.

The first 10 years after the war, 1945-1955, was the equivalent time span to the years 1919-1929, after the First World War. They were however very different periods. The twenties had been a reckless age of fortunes made and lost, with the contrast of growing unemployment for the masses and good time living for the well off who enjoyed the wild dance crazes, and adopted revolutionary new fashions. Life after the Second World War, however, was taken more seriously, purposeful reconstruction and improved living standards for the majority took place against the background of the Cold War. The atmosphere was not conducive to daring skimpy fashions and frivolous behaviour, and the new more lively post-war era started in the mid fifties, far later than before, and lasted for nearly 20 years.

In 1955 America was half way through its second decade of expansion and material affluence. Most of the younger generation had never known anything but a comfortable standard of living and liberally-minded parents, and some became dissatisfied with this rather complacent way of life. They developed new less conventional attitudes and their new attitudes were reflected in popular music and dress.

Popular singers in the early fifties like Frankie Laine and Johnny Ray, specialised in sentimental ballards, and Johnny Ray frequently dissolved into sobs and tears during his singing. In the mid fifties an insistent beat sound became the basis of the new 'Rock and Roll' music that revolutionised pop music. Bill Haley's 'Shake, Rattle and Roll', and 'Rock around the clock' charged a whole generation with an inexhaustable energy for dancing. Dance floors were filled with brightly-coloured skirts twirling out with every turn, pony-tails swung, and flat shoes ('flatties') tapped out the beat. Boys swinging the girls through turns were dressed in loose shirts or big sweaters and narrow trousers or tight blue jeans.

The rock singers became the new popular idols, they enjoyed an even greater and more demonstrative following than filmstars. Elvis Presley was the greatest of the new stars, he presented an overtly sexy image that was quite new in male singers. He wore slightly western-type clothes with shirts in bright patterns or strong plain colours edged in contrasting braiding or fringing, widely belted tight trousers, jeans and cowboy boots or crepe sole suede shoes. He immortalised his style of shoes in his famous song 'Blue suede shoes' and the words 'You can do anything but don't tread on my blue suede shoes'. During his singing Elvis often thrust his hips forward or rotated his pelvis and because of this was sometimes called 'Elvis the Pelvis'. In an early interview he was reported as saying 'I don't know what I've got but I sure hope I keep it'.

The earthier or macho type of young man was also portrayed by the film heroes. Marlon Brando in the *The Wild One* and James Dean in *Rebel Without a Cause* both slouched, snarled and mumbled their way through their roles, they played misunderstood anti-establishment characters known as crazy, mixed-up kids. They made a big impression on the young generation and their style of dressing, leather motorbike style jackets, T-shirts, blue jeans and boots, took on first in America and later in Europe, and it is a style that still appeals to young people today, over 25 years later.

Britain had taken a long time to recover from the war, but by the mid fifties was enjoying

Conventional and conservative children's hair styles and clothes carried on well into the fifties.

a prosperous spell. Upper-class social life had been revived in a simplified form, debutantes 'came out' when they were presented to the Queen at Buckingham Palace garden parties, and they held their own coming-out balls and attended their friends deb dances. English *Vogue* and *Harpers Bazaar* showed pages of clothes for the 'London season' in much the same way as they had done in the thirties. Different outfits were considered suitable for each occasion – tailored summer clothes for watching tennis on the centre court at Wimbledon, a dressy town outfit for the opening of the Royal Academy Art Show and very feminine hats and dresses for the Henley Regatta and Ascot week. London had its own couture designers called 'the top twelve'. They did not set new lines with the same authority as Paris but they catered very successfully for the social life of their customers.

Many of Britain's younger generation, like their American counterparts, were questioning accepted values, and anti-establishment ideas were coming from the more aggressive young working classes rather than dissatisfied children of the middle classes, as they were in America. John Osborne's play *'Look Back in Anger'* pin-pointed the antagonism between the classes. Working-class boys were forming the British rock and skiffle groups and universities and art colleges were filled with many more students from modest backgrounds.

Art schools and colleges were turning out well trained designers. The Royal College of Art fashion school gained a good professional reputation and its ex-students began to make their names as good designers in the wholesale clothing industry. Madge Garland started the department in the late forties and steadily built up its reputation during the first half of the fifties. She managed to elevate the fashion training to a much higher level than any other previous form of training. The late Janey Ironside took over the school in 1956. During her 12 years as principal she encouraged her students to develop their individual styles of designing.

The 'sack dress', the new unfitted line in 1957, showing the tapered skirt shortened to just below the knee.

Classic court shoes were the predominant styles of the decade. The front shoe shows the moderate shape of the early fifties, the stiletto heel and pointed toe were worn from the middle of the decade onwards.

England enjoyed its world-famous designer cult, and many of the best known designers of the sixties were ex-Royal College of Art students.

One young designer who was not an ex-fashion school student but who was to become one of the best known names of the sixties was Mary Quant. In the mid fifties she and her husband opened a small modern looking shop in London's Kings Road called 'Bazaar' where they sold simple slightly advanced looking designs which were less formal than the constructed couture clothes but more interesting than most of the mass produced styles. The Kings Road in the 1950s was an ordinary high street full of family shops, Bazaar was the first of hundreds of boutiques that transferred the Kings Road into the mecca of trendy young fashion shops during the sixties.

The new vitality in fashion designing was also affecting Italy – the Italians have always been fashion conscious with their inbred sense of style and colour. In the first half of the century although they had many good dressmakers and tailors they followed the Paris fashion lead. This began to change and for the first time since the Renaissance Italy became established as an important fashion centre. Couture and casual wear collections were presented twice a year at the Pitti Palace in Florence and each season the fashion press covered the shows in the same way as the Paris collections, apart from the pleasure of seeing the fashions in such a wonderful setting they found Italian designers inventive and progressive. The couturiers, in

The
1950s

America's famous model Suzy Parker wearing a colourful Italian printed shirt and toning tapered trousers.

particular Simonetta, her husband Fabiani, and Irene Galatzine, soon developed an international following for their elegant individual styles, but the areas where the Italians made greatest impact were in casual clothes, accessories and meanswear.

Knitwear, shirts, trousers and skirts had been adopted as important everyday clothes in America during the forties. With the more informal way of life in Europe after the war, interchangeable separates became increasingly popular. Italian designers developed them as a part of the fashion scene, new styles and themes were introduced each season.

Casual clothes followed the general silhouette of the time but they were less tightly fitted. Colourful stripes and prints were used for shirts tucked into full skirts and dresses cut with easy shirt bodices. Stoles became a very popular fashion, and were made out of the same fabrics as the dresses or in contrasting coloured knitted or woven materials. Mohair stoles in pastel shades were worn with day and evening outfits. Trousers and tops were one of the most successful styles for resort wear and all informal occasions. Trouser outfits were loose topped – big sweaters and cardigans with full sleeves pushed up, or shirts and overblouses – and were teamed with narrow tightly fitted tapered trousers. Calf-length pedal pushers were still popular but the smartest trouser line finished just above the ankle with short slits at the side.

Italian shirt and trouser outfits were often made in brightly coloured silks. Splashy printed

Marilyn Monroe's hip wiggle was adopted by many young women.

Audrey Hepburn's fawn-like looks and fringed hairstyle was widely copied.

tops and plain toning coloured trousers in orange and pink, or scarlet and emerald green, were the kind of exciting colour combinations the Italians became famous for. Women started to wear silk trouser sets for informal evenings and dressed them up with earrings, necklaces, bracelets and gold slippers. Many more women were spending holidays in Italy, the South of France and Spain and the warm summer evenings suited the colourful and casual style of dressing.

Shoes in the first half of the fifties were rather conventional in design compared to earlier and later periods. Court shoes, strappy sandals and flat ballet pumps were the main basic styles. Italian shoes had an extra elegance and refinement in shape and design. Toe and heel shapes became more pointed during the second half of the decade and toes were elongated into 'winkle-picker' points and very high heels were tapered into knife sharp stilettos. Chiropodists continually lamented a fashion which was so bad for the feet, all to no avail for toe-crippling winkle-pickers and hazardously thin stilettos became ever more popular. Permanent dents were left in floors and cracking heels became a familiar sound in city streets. Heel repair bars enjoyed a booming business.

Italy produced some of the best handbags. Soft leather and suede was used for classic square shapes with handles, flat envelope bags, and casual shoulder hanging styles with inventive looking straps and fastenings.

Important new men's fashions were introduced in Italy during the mid and late fifties. Suits were cut with the new silhouette, quite different from the English Edwardian style. Shoulders were wide-looking but not squarely padded like the American footballers' shoulders of the

Classy looking Grace Kelly wearing a popular casual outfit – silk shirt, belted waistline and tapered trousers.

forties. Sleeves were set into a slightly extended shoulder line, the width at the top was emphasised with small high fastening revers and narrow square-ended ties. The jackets hung boxy and straight and were several inches shorter than the usual man's length, they were short enough to show part of the seat and were often called 'bum starvers'. Trousers were close fitting and tapered down the leg to 16 or 17in bottoms where they broke in a fold on pointed toed shoes. Winkle-pickers were as popular for young men's shoes as they were for womens.

Italian haircuts were short and neat looking, and were razor cut to an even all-over length rather than the heavy topped floppy styles popular in England.

The Italian style became the new international trend in men's fashions. It was a younger more contemporary and less class-conscious style, and fashionable young men in Europe and America identified themselves with the first really modern post-war style for men. The new fashions were received with the least enthusiasm by conservatively-minded English men who thought it was an over slick continental style.

Chanel, who had been one of the most influential designers before the Second World War and had done much to bring in the easy fitting clothes of the twenties, reopened her fashion house in the mid fifties. In an interview just before this she expressed her views on fashion, strongly ridiculing the current styles of the time with their boned bodices and tight waists as retrograde and unsuited to the modern world. She was proved to be right although her first collections were not very well received by the press – her designs looked too much like those of the thirties. During the next few years she got back into her stride as a designer and her

Read → HERE'S HOLLYWOOD! by SIDNEY SKOLSKY

Screen stories

DELL MAGAZINE · MAY · 20¢

"RHAPSODY"

Elizabeth Taylor
Vittorio Gassman
John Ericson

Elizabeth Taylor's sultry looks and curved figure was the glamorous ideal for many people.

flattering easy fitting lines became for a second time a major fashion influence.

Perhaps sensing the social changes other couture designers began to show slightly younger easier fitting clothes. Between 1955 and 1958 a new silhouette evolved. Hairstyles became a little more contrived, long hair was still brushed smoothly back from the face but it was higher and fuller looking. The hair was folded down the back of the crown and pinned under in a 'french pleat'; it was easy to arrange and versions of the style remained popular for many years. Shorter hair styles were also cut to give a higher, fuller look rather like a flower shape – they were sometimes called the 'chrysanthemum cut'. Hats followed the higher line with drum and cossack shapes. In the spring issues of the fashion magazines in 1956 there were many features on the new 'hatty hats', they were feminine looking toques made in draped chiffon or organdie and trimmed with roses and veiling, similar to the styles worn just before the First World War. They were popular with mature fashion conscious women but rarely worn by the younger generation.

Shoulder lines were natural and unexaggerated but no longer deliberately sloped. The semi-fitted shape, collarless or with a stand-away collar had become the predominant line for suits and coats. Fitted tops and full skirts were still popular for dresses but some of the higher fashion styles followed the same easy fit as the jackets with flattish unwaisted bodices and narrow tapered skirts. In his autumn collection in 1956, Balenciaga emphasised the new dress line by shortening the skirt length to the top of the calf.

The 1957 autumn fashion shows confirmed the unfitted line and much shorter skirts, the new length varied from the top of the calf to just below the knee – it was the shortest length for over a decade. Ten years after Dior's 'New Look' the fashionable shape for women had once again changed. Small, tightly fitted tops and full, long skirts were replaced by loose tops

The
1950s

In 1959 girls all over the world tried to look like Brigitte Bardot with her pouting mouth and cascading hairstyle.

and narrow brief skirts. The scanty post-war styles that had been predicted by the fashion historian James Laver had arrived at last.

The new dress line was called 'the sack'. Shops were quickly filled with inexpensive versions of the new style, and women rushed to buy their 'sack dresses', which they wore with long rows of pearls or toning coloured beads in the style of the 1920s. There was, however, a subtle but noticeable difference between shapeless dresses with side seams and bust darts and the more expensive well cut dresses where the bust and waist was cleverly indicated with darts and seams. A well cut sack or chemise dress was quite an attractive line, it moved with the female form gently shadowing the lines of the figure.

Enforced school uniforms and conventional conservative clothes for boys and girls carried on well into the fifties. But miniature versions of the teenage styles began to be adapted for children. Girls loved their hair pulled into pony-tails. They also liked full-skirted cotton print dresses with petticoats which swung out like their older sisters' as they jigged to rock and roll music. Loose shirts and sweaters in stripes or strong plain colours were teamed with toning pedal-pushers and flat pumps to make practical colourful outfits for weekends and holidays. Bright casual clothes were also being worn more by boys out of school hours and knitted shirts and jeans had become standard.

Synthetic fibres like Terylene, Acrilan, Bri-Nylon and Orlon were on the market by the late fifties. Mothers found they were a boon, reinforced nylon socks did away with hours of darning and the easy care and shape-retaining qualities of the new children's clothes meant they could be washed in the local launderette or family washing machine.

By 1958 fashion had become more international, influences on dress were wider, and the way fashion was set and followed began to change. The Paris couturiers were still a major influence, and buyers and press habitually attended the twice yearly shows, but the authority of the designers had lessened, new lines did not have quite the same impact and their dictatorial powers were beginning to wane.

In the spring collections for 1958 the successful sack dress was developed into two far less popular lines – 'the oval' and the 'trapeze'. The oval shape was the sack front with a blown-out balloon-shaped back. The trapeze slightly shaped the figure under the bust, bypassed the waist and flared out to quite a wide width round the hem. It looked rather like a maternity dress and some women in fact wore them for that purpose. Neither of the new lines had much success in the important mass market. Sack dresses in beige, pale lemon and white linen were far more popular, particularly in France and Italy.

Many women, however, still thought of the unfitted dress as an alternative shape and were not ready to give up dresses with tight bodices and very full skirts. Clothing manufacturers realised that there was still a receptive market for this well-established style and although contrary to the new Paris lines, full skirted dresses over stiffened petticoats shortened to just below the knee cap continued to sell well for the next two years. Women had become more confident about wearing the styles they liked.

Although skirts were still sold in far larger quantities, trousers were gaining in popularity every year with the younger market. Well-fitting tapered trousers, in tartan wool and twill fabrics in the winter and cotton gaberdine or linen in the summer, had become basic garments in many women's wardrobes. They were still never worn in offices or fashionable restaurants but they were quite acceptable for casual weekend wear or informal evenings at home.

Teenage clothes were an important part of fashion. The new styles and shorter skirts were thought to be very suitable for the young market. Some teenagers felt the clothes were too commercial and wanted their own styles that they could intuitively want to wear rather than styles that reflected older people's ideas of how they thought young people should dress. Some of the young generation felt unhappy about the way they saw society developing; it was considered too materialistic with a risk of mass destruction in a possible war. 'Ban the Bomb' marches became a feature of the late fifties, and young men and women marched considerable distances dressed in big sweaters, duffle coats and dark trousers or jeans.

Vaguely anti-establishment views were often held by the more style conscious 'beats' or 'beatniks'. They had their own expressions – 'squares' were the more conventional members of society, friends who reacted too emotionally to situations were told to 'cool it' and possible converts to a more 'beat' style of dressing were told to 'get with it'. The beatnik style for girls consisted of a loosely arranged backcombed hairstyle, pinned or held with a horseshoe-shaped metal slide and prong into a deliberately untidy french pleat, or the hair was worn long and loose on the shoulders. Faces were paled and eyes heavily emphasised with sooty-looking eye make-up, oversized pullovers and short tight skirts in dark colours, or mattress-ticking dresses in grey and black, were worn with black stockings and stilettos or long boots in squashy black leather.

The 'beat' style for men appears moderate in retrospect. Hair was un-set but comparatively short, clothes were dark coloured – black pullovers and sombre flannel shirts went with black or grey denim or cord jeans and black leather jackets or waistcoats. It was a fairly unremarkable style by later standards but at the time when many people, particularly the

One of Slimma's early trouser suits in 1959. The model's short hair followed the trend for a fuller blown-up effect.

Swimwear became briefer and better fitting.

older generation, had very set views on men dressing in a gentlemanly way beatniks represented the anti-establishment and a disrespect for the conventional way of life.

Filmstars looks, figures and mannerisms still exerted a big influence on women's appearance. Marilyn Monroe combined a very appealing mixture of vulnerability and naughtiness, and the Marilyn Monroe walk with its hip wiggle was copied by many girls. Elizabeth Taylor and Ava Gardner with their dark sultry looks and fashionably rounded figures represented the ideal in fifties glamour for many people.

Grace Kelly and Audrey Hepburn's refinement and elegance epitomised the cool classy looks of the time. The clothes for many of Audrey Hepburn's films were designed by Givenchy one of the successful new designers. Her Givenchy clothes in *Sabrina Fair* and *Funny Face* were some of the best high-fashion film clothes of the period. Audrey Hepburn's short hairstyle and irregularly-shaped fringe was also admired and copied.

European film stars like Italy's Sophia Loren and Gina Lollobrigida, with their natural looks, curvy figures and earthier sex appeal suited the freer attitudes many young men and women were adopting.

But the strongest influence on young women's looks came from France's Brigitte Bardot. She had become internationally famous after her role in the film *Woman was Created* in which she played a young temptress. In the film reviews she was described as a 'sex kitten';

during the late fifties and early sixties provocative young starlets were often called 'sex kittens'.

Brigitte Bardot enjoyed the casual beach life in the South of France and was regularly photographed showing off her well proportioned figure in very brief bikinis. These now used considerably less material, and French styles were known for their extremely good fit. Girls in their late teens and early twenties tried hard to look like Bardot. Hair was put into a style of contrived disarray, the front was backcombed into a high soft beehive, the back and sides cascaded into soft waves and curls. Eyes were heavily made up but lips were painted a whitish pink with 'young pink lipstick'.

The short pink and white gingham dress trimmed with broderie anglaise that Bardot wore for her second marriage in 1959 was copied by many clothing manufacturers and home dressmakers, and gingham became the craze fabric of the summer.

England enjoyed an unusually long hot summer in 1959, the Prime Minister Harold McMillan said 'you've never had it so good'. People were certainly more prosperous and holidays abroad, well equipped homes, cars and television sets had become commonplace. Fashionable clothes were worn by young people of all classes, and Europe was catching up with affluent American living standards. A new generation had grown up who could hardly remember the war or the post-war austerity years. They wanted their own fashions and were developing definite ideas on what they wanted, very different from the conservative ladylike and gentlemanly styles of the earlier fifties.

By the end of the decade, young cult fashions, the beatniks and 'ton-up' styles were being adapted by the more advanced couturiers like Saint Laurent, the idea of lower-class fashions being refined for upper-class wear was unique in the history of fashion. It was, however, just the beginning of a whole cycle of youth-oriented fads and cults which were to change the structure of fashion during the 'Swinging Sixties'.

The
1960s

'The Swinging Sixties' and 'The Roaring Twenties' have already gone into history as the fun periods of the century. They were the only decades to be given names that instantly conveyed the lighter side of life. In many ways they were akin to one another. They both experienced expansion, major social changes, daring young fashions and new styles in popular music and dancing. In the twenties the middle and upper classes had instigated and taken part in the changes. The social revolution of the sixties was more extensive. Ideas came from all classes, and fashion was followed by a wider range of young people than ever before.

Although styles had become younger looking during the late fifties, the clothes illustrated in the fashion magazines at the beginning of the 1960s still looked mature and conventional compared to the designs of a few years later. Fashions with a recognisably sixties look took a few years to establish themselves.

The sixties 'Dolly Girl' in her mini-skirt, like the twenties flapper, in her knee-length dress, did not represent fashion throughout the decade. In both cases the new shortness in skirts applied to the middle and later years.

In 1920 calf-length skirts were considered the ultimate in brevity. Within five years hemlines had reached an unprecedented knee length. An exact parallel took place 40 years later. The sixties began with skirts about as short as the shortest lengths of the twenties. Hems were as high as most people thought they could be. By the middle of the decade the thigh-length mini had arrived and a new record in shortness had been achieved.

Fashion conscious women had adopted higher, fuller hair styles by 1960, and a blown up air-filled effect continued to be used by many women throughout the decade, despite regular fashion reports informing women that it was no longer fashionable. Backcombing was an everyday part of arranging hair. Most styles were based on a beehive or birds nest front and to add still more height some styles, particularly for evening wear, crowned the beehive with a top-knot or a group of curls. The added top pieces were sometimes made of false hair. Hair dressers training in the early sixties remember being allowed to arrange some of the clients' styles. They were sometimes told that although the hair had been well done the client felt it wasn't high enough. Other styles had a hard beehive front and long back hair falling from the top of the crown to the shoulders where it turned out in a 'flick-up'. To hold the contrived styles in position they were sprayed with hair lacquer which tended to make them stiff and immobile.

Set blown-up hair was easily dinted by hat wearing. By the early sixties most younger women only wore hats for special occasions. Hats were designed to complement and accommodate the high hair styles, they had deep roomy crowns or they were small pill-box shapes attached to the back of the built-up hair. The American President's wife popularised this style and hats like the ones she wore were often called 'Jackie Kennedy pill-boxes'.

Casual interchangeable separates were becoming increasingly popular with younger women. But tailored clothes with gloves and classic square-shaped handbags and dresses with varying degrees of formality still formed the basic garments in many women's wardrobes. Suits and coats in tweeds and wool gaberdine were strongly influenced by the severely elegant style Balenciaga had developed in the fifties. They had stand-away necklines and straight or semi-fitted body shapes. Three or four large fancy buttons in pearl, metal or draped silk were the eye-catching features of many of the designs. Very narrow tapered skirts were still worn but

Fashionable clothes at the beginning of the sixties still looked conventional with neat hats and gloves. Jackie Kennedy in 1962 wearing a Chanel style suit and a pill-box hat on the back of her full hair style.

Formal evening dresses followed the lines of the late fifties with fitted bodices and bell-shaped skirts.

Fitted bodices and full skirts like this bridesmaid's dress were still popular in the early sixties. The Italian style man's suit had narrow tapered trousers.

Blown-up hair had added height with top-knots and curls.

the newer easier shapes were straight and lightly gathered into the waistband or cut in panels to give a gently flared line at the hem.

The most successful new suit style of the time was the 'Chanel suit'. After a rather shaky start Chanel steadily rebuilt her reputation as a creative designer. By the early sixties she was firmly re-established and enjoying publicity and acclaim for her easy fitted suits. They were less austere looking than the other couturiers' designs and suited women of all ages. Chanel used soft handling woollens and tweeds lightly interlined and attractively edged with fancy wool or silk braiding, usually in contrasting colours. The jackets were often worn open, some of them were cut edge to edge without buttoned fastenings but held together with a brooch shaped clip. The suits were matched or toned to silky blouses with scarf collars or neck-bands that tied into floppy bows. Skirts were cut with easy straightish lines and pockets in the front panels or the side seams.

To complete the total Chanel look specially designed Chanel handbags with chain handles were carried and flattering shoes with black leather or silk toe-caps and beige suede uppers with sling backs were worn. Hair was cut in a soft fringe and sometimes tied back with a neat black silk ribbon. The Chanel style was feminine and appealing. Wholesale manufacturers copied her designs in all price ranges and it became one of the most commercial styles of the time. Britain's Wallis shops produced some of the best and most reasonably priced versions and became well known for their 'Chanel Suits'.

Dress shapes were quite varied. Tight bodices and full skirts lingered on into the first year or two of the decade, but the easy unfitted line was gaining in popularity. It was a slightly more shaped version of the late fifties 'sack', re-named the 'shift'. The bust and the waist

Jean Shrimpton one of the new young models of the early sixties, her hair was slightly raised over the crown.

were lightly indicated and the skirt shape was straight rather than tapered. Sleeveless, knee-length shift dresses in silky evening fabrics, particularly in black, suited the hip and arm movements of the 'twist', the dance craze of 1961.

Fashion at the beginning of the decade was definitely younger, more relaxed and less dictatorial than it had been ten years before. The couture designers suggested many new ideas but they no longer presented uncompromising 'looks' and 'lines'. Fashion had to appeal to the mass market. Fit could not be too exacting and design details had to be suitable for production methods. Fashion had once again moved with the times but revolutionary new styles had yet to show themselves.

The youth orientated styles of the sixties, unlike some of the earlier important fashion changes of the century, cannot be dated to a specific year or to one designer. It was part of an international movement towards a new approach in dressing that had started in the mid-fifties and gradually gathered momentum.

By 1963 the style of the sixties had begun to emerge. The young French ready-to-wear designers were becoming known for their refreshingly informal designs. Their clothes were far less categorised. Jackets, skirts and dresses were no longer aimed at specific occasions; they had all the traditional French flair for cut and the use of fabrics. The garments were not heavily structured, and contrived lines were no longer important. Design interest was concentrated on details, the shape of collars, the unusual use of colours and material, and the way outfits were worn. Dresses were cut like easy fitting blouses and shirts with soft girlish design features. Collars were limply rounded or droopily pointed; sleeve-heads were gently gathered and sleeves flared out towards the wrists or were gathered into bands. Small pearl or

The Beatles in 1963.

bead buttons were used for fastenings or as decoration. The soft limp designs were reminiscent of the early thirties but the unwaisted fit and knee-length skirts gave the new style dresses a child-like appearance which was further emphasised by the use of small flower-printed fabrics. England's well known Liberty prints were often used for these young looking dresses.

In contrast to frilly feminine styles, trousers and trouser outfits were becoming more popular. Trouser sales soared and trouser shapes and styles developed their own fashions. They were no longer confined to one basic shape as they had been in the forties and fifties. Narrow tapered trousers were still a popular line but the more fashion conscious styles were cut to finish on the top of the hips rather than into the waistline. Varying widths of belt were slotted through the trouser belt loops so that they sat low down like cowboy pants. They were called 'hipsters' and as an alternative to narrow trouser legs, flared bell bottoms were introduced. Hipsters were often made in denim or cotton twill and teamed with boyish denim shirts, giving a rather 'Western look'. The cowboy style was featured in fashion photographs. Young men and women were pictured in similar shirts, waistcoats, hipster trousers or hipster jeans, neck scarves and stetson hats. It was the first of the many Western crazes that became a recurring fashion theme during the next 20 years.

Tight jeans showing off figures, had become an accepted although not universally worn fashion in the mid-fifties. Skin-tight jeans became more popular in the early sixties. Young people in their teens and early twenties shrank their jeans on them in the bath. They were labelled 'guaranteed to shrink and fade'. They were scrubbed to give the seat and legs a deliberately worn and faded look. Jeans were often so tight they could only be zipped closed by lying on the floor.

Stretch trousers made from wool and helanca or wool and Bri-nylon became an extremely commercial style. To emphasise the slim line they were made with a stirrup-shaped fabric loop attached to the bottoms of the trousers. The loops slipped under the sole of the foot pulling the legs straight down from the seat rather than clinging to the hips and thighs. Many women thought it was a more flattering line. Slimma, the well known British women's trouser firm, sold stretch trousers in large quantities for several years.

Resort clothes were a growing influence on casual wear. St Tropez in the South of France became the centre where many of the young fashion crazes for men and women originated. The crowded boutiques round the old port launched new styles in fabrics, colours, trouser shapes, shirts and swimwear each year. The 'in' style of the season was quickly evident. Sun-

Girls with beehive hair styles and boys with Beatle fringes in Liverpool's famous Cavern.

tanned young people in the latest tops and trousers paraded about or lounged in the harbourside cafés confidently displaying the right look. A pale new arrival, not wearing the season's 'St Trop' style, often felt dowdily unattractive!

St Tropez was at the peak of its popularity as the most fashionable Mediterranean resort in the early and mid-sixties. Clothing manufacturers from all over the world paid annual visits to absorb the new trends and enjoy a pleasant stay in the colourful and exciting atmosphere of the town and the nearby beaches and possibly catch a glimpse of Brigitte Bardot or other members of the glamorous jet set. New lines and ideas were discussed and future wholesale ranges were planned on the Tahiti beach.

Trousers and shirts in the same fabrics and colours were worn by men and women. The press started to talk about 'unisex' fashions. Women going on holiday to the South of France sometimes only took swimwear and shirts and trousers. Dresses were not fashionable in the younger trendier resorts. Although trouser wearing had become the dominant style, women began to feel they would like to wear something to keep their legs cool and less confined. One of the new attractive fashions in 1963 were the thigh length beach dresses and shirts worn over bikinis for wandering about the town at lunchtime or in the early evening. The new tops looked young and modern. They were the forerunners of the mini dresses.

Leather jackets, waistcoats and long boots had been considered a beatnik style in the late fifties. During the early sixties leather was developed into a wider range of fashion garments, soft supple skins in more extensive colour ranges were used for cardigans, topcoats, skirts and pinafore dresses as well as the casual all-purpose leather jackets which had become basic garments for many young men and women. Although leather was admired, many people were still rather inhibited and self-conscious about wearing what was often called 'kinky leather gear'. Widish, squashy, knee-length boots with varying heel heights and pointed or squared-off toes, were also sometimes known as 'kinky boots'. Boots suited the more extrovert young style of dressing and although shapes have altered and the press have suggested that they might be going out of fashion from time to time, boot wearing has been an established part of fashion for 20 years.

Synthetic fabrics were developed with a shiny look and a leather texture. Jackets and coats made in the new fibres were far less expensive than real leather. They became very popular for mass-produced garments and they were usually described in magazines as the 'wet look'.

England and particularly London, which America's *TIME* magazine christened 'Swinging London', enjoyed an international reputation for its lively young generation. Britain had its

SPÉCIAL PAQUES

LES DRAMES
D'UNE FEMME TROMPÉE

LA MODE
" PETITES FLEURS "

Dresses with their unwaisted fit had a very young,
almost childlike, appearance.

own highly successful pop singers and groups but Liverpool's 'Beatles' propelled British talent to the forefront of international pop music. They took the world by storm in 1963 and 1964. There were scenes of adulation and mass-hysteria from teenagers wherever they appeared and 'Beatlemania' swept round the world in less than two years. Apart from their music and singing, girls liked the way the group looked and boys quickly copied their style. The Beatles' hair cut with its straight across the forehead fringe was copied by countless young men. Their slim-fitting, high fastening or collarless suits and jackets also became very fashionable. The Beatles wore ankle-covering elastic-sided boots; boots like the ones they wore were already popular with style-conscious young men, and were called 'Chelsea Boots'. They were soon renamed 'Beatle Boots', and queues formed outside shops as new stocks of what were reputed to be exact copies of the Beatles' styles arrived from the manufacturers. Parents were sometimes surprised to see their sons wearing old-fashioned looking elastic-sided boots and innocent enquiries were sometimes made as to whether their sons had developed weak ankles!

Britain's young fashion designers spurred on by Mary Quant's success with her inventive and uninhibited designs developed their own exciting individual styles. Buyers from all over the world included a stop in London on their bi-annual European trips. They found the London styles refreshingly youthful and inexpensive. Some designers' ranges were off-shoots of large, well-established clothing manufacturers. Others went into business on their own. They started their firms with great enthusiasm. Unfortunately lack of capital and experience in

Boys shirts and 'hipster' trousers became a very popular young fashion.

running a clothing company sometimes impeded designing talent and progress. However, some of the new young names of the sixties went on to greater things and are well respected and established today, 20 years later. Jean Muir, Janice Wainwright and John Bates are some of the best known names.

By 1964 the swinging image of the decade was under way. Youthful energetic pop music and unconventional less class-conscious clothes were a form of universal communication amongst the young.

The Paris couture designers continued to produce elegant beautifully made clothes in top quality fabrics but they no longer had the authority to change the direction in which fashion was going. This trend was temporarily reversed by the impact of a new designer, André Courréges.

Courréges had trained with Balenciaga, and during the early sixties he started his own small couture house. He quickly gained a reputation for his advanced looking designs. They were clearly influenced by Balenciaga's severe elegance but they looked more modern. Courréges in his autumn 1964 collection caused a sensation. It was the most dramatic couture change since Dior's legendary 'New Look' in 1947. The Courréges designs were stark and modern but also exciting. They looked like a glimpse into the future, and were a reflection of the great interest in space exploration during the sixties.

He presented his collection in plain white showrooms. His models were tall and impressively athletic looking. They were suntanned white girls or glowing black models. The clothes were

Mary Quant in the dark glasses photographed with a selection of her Ginger Group range in 1963.

Courrèges introduced his futuristic designs in 1964. The styles were modified by wholesale manufacturers.

Vidal Sassoon finishing one of his styles cut into an even manageable length.

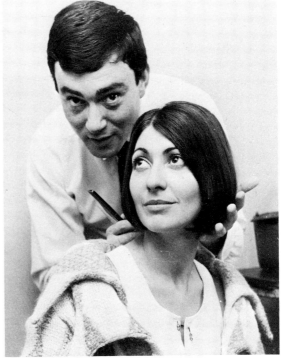

flattish with an only slight indication of the figure, and to give their precise sculptured shape he used heavy wool crepe or gaberdine in dramatic-looking white, bright red or strong green. Hair was very short and cropped or scraped tightly back. Hats were helmet shaped; they were either worn straight on top of the head with high domed crowns or they wrapped around the head and tied under the chin in a neat firm bow. Shoulder lines were wide and rounded. Design details were carefully proportioned and balanced. Stand-away collars, pockets and top-stitched seams were always immaculately tailored.

Many of his outfits included trousers. They were cleverly cut with centre front seams giving a long elegant and controlled line that flared out slightly over the top of the feet and opened into short front slits showing the specially designed calf-length Courréges boots worn under the trousers. When Courréges put skirts with his outfits his lengths were several inches above the knee and they were worn with boots not shoes. His famous boots were in soft white kid or strong bright colours. They were zipped up the inside and the toe shapes were squared off. They became one of the most widely copied boot styles of the century.

Although thigh-length hemlines had been worn for resort wear and some young British designers had daringly shown skirts just above the knee-cap, Courréges was the first designer to launch the mini confidently and uncompromisingly as the only correct day length. He formally introduced the mini skirt to the fashion world. It was the most important development of the decade.

Courréges's clothes, like earlier fashions, when they were first introduced were too extreme for most women, but his space-age style was modified and adapted by other designers and wholesale manufacturers and his clean-cut lines and clear colours became one of the major influences of the mid and late sixties.

Many women's initial reaction to the mini skirt was that they would never wear it. However, the young generation loved it and throughout 1965 and 1966 skirts got shorter and shorter. Some of the shortest minis were worn in London and they were sometimes called 'pelmets'.

Quite conservative manufacturers lopped inches off hemlines every season. In the early sixties Slimma's average skirt lengths had been 25 or 26in from the waist to just below the knee. By 1966 an 18in overall length was quite unremarkable for bulk production lines.

Older women in their fifties and sixties also shortened their skirts slightly each year. Grandmothers were soon wearing the shortest skirt lengths they had ever known.

As an alternative to mini skirts and mini dresses, trouser suits started to be worn. Classic blazers and Courréges inspired double-breasted reefer jackets in flannel and gaberdine became fashionable town outfits. Women wore them with stetson-shaped hats, cravat necked blouses, jewellery, gloves and dressy looking patent leather shoes or boots. Evening suits were made in velvet or black wool crepe. Wearing trouser suits to fashionable restaurants and race meetings like Ascot was still considered very advanced and some restaurants at first refused admission to women in trouser outfits. There was quite a lot of publicity about trouser suit wearing and yet within a couple of years they were accepted for almost any occasion, day or evening, and young women started wearing them in offices.

By 1966 a new approach to fashionable dressing had become established. The mature woman was no longer admired. Fashion catered exclusively to the young. Older women complained that their age group was ignored by the progressive designers. The styles of the mid-sixties certainly looked their best on girls in their late teens and early twenties.

There were two popular ways of looking and dressing. The boyish sporty look, and the dolly girl style. England's teenage model Twiggy epitomised the boyish look. She had very short straight hair in an updated version of the 1920s pudding basin cut but fuller and less hard looking. Vidal Sassoon became famous for his skillful cutting. He broke away from heavily lacquered beehive styles. Hair was cleverly shaped and layered into an even overall length. It was sculptured and yet soft. Hair was easy to manage and it kept its shape. Mary Quant adopted the Vidal Sassoon cut with a schoolgirl fringe and has continued to wear a version of the style up to the present day.

Sandy Shaw, one of the popular young women singers of the time, often barefoot for stage and television shows, had very well cut hair which moved beautifully while she sang and danced and always fell perfectly back into place.

With the neat short hair styles, very simple dresses were worn. They were based on a T-shirt shape and made in knitted stripes or strong plain colours with a contrasting collar and a short front opening like a football shirt. Other styles were collarless, long sleeved in the winter, and short sleeves or sleeveless in the summer. Dresses bypassed the waist and finished anywhere from the middle of the thighs to three or four inches above the knee. With the establishment of the mini, tights had replaced stockings and they were often textured with ribs and fancy patterns. Cream tights were sometimes worn with dark clothes and shoes.

David Bond's trouser suit for Slimma was worn with an evening handbag and shoes.

Herringbone designs and stripes also focused interest on the legs. Some manufacturers tried to sell dresses and skirts with matching tights but it usually proved to be too difficult to package and market.

The boyish style with short hair, T-shirt dress and fancy patterned tights was completed with long boots or flat or medium heeled shoes. Pointed and chiselled toes and thin heels had carried on well into the sixties but the shapes didn't suit the athletic looking mini styles. Shoes became chunkier with thicker, lower heels and rounded or squared toes. Buckle shoes in patent became very fashionable and some styles were made with silver or gold coloured heels to match the buckles.

Britain's well known photographic models like Jean Shrimpton and Pattie Boyd presented a more feminine or 'Dolly Girl' image. Hair was slightly raised in the crown and then allowed to fall long and loose onto the shoulders. Long loose hair tended to fall forward onto the face. Girls developed the habit of shaking or tossing the head back to temporarily clear the face and eyes. It became a very characteristic gesture of the sixties.

Dolly girl clothes were under-sized and very young. Ribbed pullovers in pastel colours were called 'skinny ribs' and were sometimes bought in children's departments to get them as small and tight as possible. Dolly outfits were simply shaped, mini short and worn with pale lacey tights. Dresses were trimmed with frills, lace edgings and embroidered ribbons. Open-knit crocheted tops and dresses in cream or soft pastel shades were a popular alternative style. Some women produced very successful home crocheted garments, the more daring wore them without bras and underslips.

With girlish looking dresses a loose chain belt was often clipped round the top of the hips and a small quilted leather handbag hung from the shoulders on narrow chains.

Flowing manes and tiny pretty dresses were rather incongruously worn with black or white knee-length leather boots, even in the summer. The young generation happily broke all the rules about what went with what and appropriate clothes for occasions or times of the year. They wore what they felt like wearing whether it was sleeveless mini dresses in mid-winter or high boots on hot summer days.

Fashion photography became an important influence. Fashion magazines gave photographers far more scope and artistic licence. Some photographers were at least as well known as the young designers and the successful model girls. Their new approach to photographing clothes changed attitudes to fashion and the way clothes were worn. Garments were no longer posed statically on coolly elegant women neatly and formally accessorised. Many more pictures were taken in colour and on exciting locations. Editorial fashion staff and models flew all over the world to find stimulating and unusual settings. Girls were photographed running, jumping, and flying through the air. Pictures helped to create a mood, a look and the young swinging image.

Girls were less concerned about quality and the subtle evolution of cut and line. Older women pointed out that they could no longer study the details of the clothes shown in the magazines and weigh up the pros and cons of a new style before going out to buy.

The way clothes were bought changed. Young trendy boutiques, copied from the ones in London's famous Carnaby Street and Chelsea's King's Road, sprang up everywhere. Local suburbs and country towns all had their own small shops selling younger fashions. The large departmental store felt the new competition and opened young departments or shops within

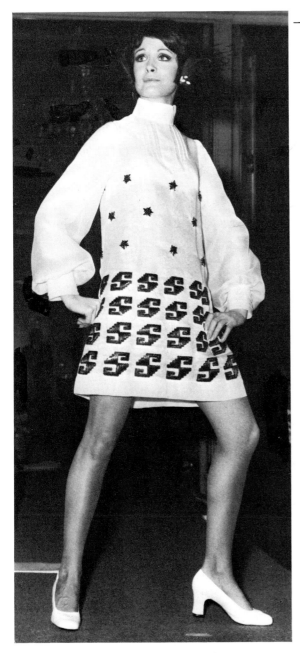

Some mid-sixties mini dresses were cut like over-
blouses and were almost see-through.

Loose dresses with pale tights were popular.

shops where manufacturers rented and stocked space in the stores. Chain stores expanded and developed a reputation second to none for quality and value.

The sixties was the most prosperous of all the decades but spending habits changed. Family incomes were spent on home improvements, colour televisions and stereo equipment. Many more homes had two cars; boats and caravans became increasingly popular and holidays abroad were enjoyed by many more people. Affluent middle-class families acquired second homes and sometimes took two or three holidays a year.

The casual, mobile life altered attitudes towards clothes. Women cared less about looking lady-like in neat tailored styles. Separates in easy-care fabrics like crimplene and Trevira became the basic everyday garments for many married women over thirty. Trousers, tops, knitwear and shirts that could be easily put in the washing machine were the commercial mass-produced clothes of the time.

Easy-care and washability became one of the most important sales features. The producers

Simple mini dresses worn with
fashionable hair styles and
prominent earrings.

of synthetic fibres spent large sums on sales promotion. Nearly all children's clothes were in
man-made fabrics. Children's clothes, like the adult styles, became more functional and
colourful. The hair styles and the lines of the sixties, like the 1920s fashions, were ideal for
children. Shift dresses worn over ribbed sweaters and matching ribbed tights suited mothers
and daughters. The proportions and lengths were exactly the same, only the scale differed.
Trousers, dungarees and zip-fronted jerkin tops in bright red and blue knitted fabrics were
worn by boys and girls. There was far less difference in the clothes worn by either sex.
Teenage and adult styles tended to merge into one. Most of the young adult fashions were
quite suitable for the teens and very few young women considered teenage clothes too
youthful for them to wear.

   During the first half of the sixties young men had lost their diffidence about showing an
obvious interest in following fashion. Men's and women's styles often followed a similar
development. Well cut hair was important to both sexes. Fashionable hairdressers cut men's
and women's hair in the same open-plan salon. It was quite a revelation to older men used to
having an inexpensive 'short back and sides' at the local high street barber.

   The same skinny rib sweaters were often shared and swopped by brothers and sisters and
girls and their boyfriends. Trouser fashions, apart from women's stretch pants with foot loops,
were based on similar lines. Many women preferred men's trousers. They liked the flat hip
fitting but found the waistlines were usually too large. Low cut hipsters solved the problem
and women bought many pairs from men's shops.

   Men's suits and jackets were still based on the Italian line of the late fifties but modified
into a longer less boxy shape giving a very slim line. The ideal figure for men was skinny and
boyish. Shirt collars were small with short points or rounded edges. White collars on checks,
stripes or plain strong coloured shirts were very fashionable. Gingham checks in black and
white and blue and white were also popular and usually worn with narrow knitted silk ties in
plain colours. Topcoats and raincoats were straight and, like the women's lengths, several
inches above the knee.

Crocheted dresses in cream or soft pastel shades were popular in the middle to late sixties.

Twiggy's adolescent thinness emphasised by the girlish mini dress.

Young women and girls wore the same styles in clothes and boots.

Mick Jagger and mini-skirted
Marianne Faithfull.

Although young men had become very style conscious, they still aimed at a neat sharp appearance. Deliberate untidiness had not yet become fashionable.

By 1967 the mood of the sixties had begun to change. The early enthusiasm and vitality waned. The dynamic young generation seemed less self-confident. The horrors of the Vietnam War were visually relayed in colour into comfortable homes and often complacently accepted by the viewers. Many young people wanted to evolve a new way of living far removed from rampant materialism and cynical aggression. Drug taking increased alarmingly. Others turned to mysticism, cults and Eastern religions.

Hippies and flower-power was one of the most popular cult movements. Hippy styles of dress became an important influence. Hair for both sexes was grown to at least shoulder length and sometimes permed, or if it was naturally wavy it fell in rather unkempt curls. Narrow beaded headbands or scarves were sometimes worn across the forehead and fastened at the back in the style of the North American Indian. Shaggy beards and moustaches were very popular for men. Girls often wore flowers in their hair and apart from a little eye make-up faces were natural and serene or dreamy facial expressions were cultivated.

Jewellery was worn in great quantities. Rows of Eastern looking beads hung round necks, bracelets jangled at the wrists and several rings were worn on the fingers of both hands.

Indian made shirts and over-blouses in cheesecloth were embroidered with flowers and beads and worn with loose tunics and waistcoats. Plain or patterned sheepskin-lined Afghan style jackets were popular in the winter.

Some girls wore loose flowing floor-length kaftans edged with braiding and embroidery and

Hippie in embroidered over-shirt
with London policeman.

Hippies handing out flowers at the
Woburn Abbey rally in 1967.

Elegant high fashion evening dresses
influenced by the hippie styles.

Model girl version of the freak-out hair style.

frequently worn without shoes even for walks along city streets. Trousers were very tight fitting over the hips but widely flared at the hem. They were sometimes tucked into rather scuffed suede boots with turned back fringed tops like the ones worn by Indian scouts in Western films. Other boots were made of multi-coloured leather or suede patchwork. Many hippies preferred sandals or soft slippers.

Pop stars like the Beatles changed from their smart clean-cut appearance of the early sixties and adopted a rather hippie style with longer more careless hair and loose shirts and waistcoats. Many of their later songs had social messages and deeper meanings. The Rolling Stones, Britain's equally successful group of the mid and late sixties, captured the disenchanted mood. Mick Jagger pranced, preened and strutted in big sleeved shirts open to the waist and skin tight satin jeans as he sang 'Can't get no satisfaction'.

Dress designers reflected the mood of the later sixties with their fantasy clothes. Britain's exciting new designer, Zandra Rhodes, had originally trained as a textile designer at the Royal College of Art. She concocted wonderful combinations of prints and fabrics which she made into billowing kaftan style dresses which were cut with the sleeves and the bodice all in one to give a huge batwing effect when the models spread out their arms. Sweeping arm movements were often used at fashion shows and in the photographs in the glossy magazines like *Vogue* and *Harper's Bazaar*.

'The Romantic Look' was one of the strongest fashion trends in 1967 and 1968. Hair styles

Typical trendy young boutique of the later sixties. Two of the girls appear very advanced with longer 'midi' skirts.

were brushed back but a few curls were allowed to fall onto the side of the face. The back hair was tied with a ribbon at the top of the crown and waved and curled onto the shoulders. A few locks were pulled forward to hang down the front. Other styles had a mass of contrived back curls giving a wood-shaving effect. The styles looked like a cross between an 18th-century dandy and a mid 19th-century Southern belle.

Plain and crushed velvet was widely used for day and evening clothes. Jacket shapes for men and women had wide floppy collars and revers, small high armholes and body-shaped lines flaring slightly over the hips. Frilly blouses and shirts with high cravat necklines and lace ruffles down the front and round the wrists were very popular with both sexes. Men and women also wore the same type of flared trousers over high-heeled leather or suede boots. Knickerbockers were introduced to give a Little Lord Fauntleroy look. They were occasionally worn by some women but trousers were the predominant style.

Biba shops were dark looking with potted palms and plants and clothes hooked onto old coatstands.

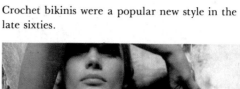

Crochet bikinis were a popular new style in the late sixties.

Maurice Attwood's 'wet look' raincoats for 'Valstar' were one of the big sellers in 1969.

Mini skirts were as popular as ever and to give a swashbuckling appearance thigh-length boots in soft kid were sometimes worn. Tights were nearly always in dark colours for the winter and to wear with velvet evening skirts and dresses. Shoes were getting noticeably heavier looking with broader thicker heels and round toes. Small platform soles were beginning to appear on some styles.

Although the mini was still riding high, longer skirts were introduced as an extra style rather than a rival to the established length. Lower calf and ankle-length fur trimmed Zhivago coats shown as early as 1966 by Dior were inspired by the successful *Dr. Zhivago* film. The style fitted in perfectly with the romantic revival. They were usually worn over minis and boots.

Mid-calf length dresses and skirts called 'midis' were less successful. Women used to showing their legs in trousers and short skirts felt the midi was rather ageing. It was a high fashion style and designers anxious for a new proportion for their designs promoted the length in 1968 and 1969, but only a few very style-conscious women wore calf-length clothes and then only as an alternative line. They were not ready to give up the mini altogether.

Biba, one of the most successful young fashion shops showed clothes in dark interesting settings.

Active sports clothes were influenced by the freer, less formalised way of dressing. The variety and scope for ski clothes developed strongly. Skiing holidays became less exclusively upper class and were enjoyed by many more people. Fashionable resorts like France's Megéve promoted the winter equivalent to St. Tropez' summer styles. Elasticated fabrics were always used for well cut ski trousers and the newer all-in-one stretch overalls. There was a wider variety of colours-pale pinks, lilacs and light blues were worn as well as the more usual reds, blues and blacks. Ski boots became more modern with protective functional shapes and strong clasp fastenings. Anoraks were available in a wide variety of styles and fabrics. Contrasting colours such as black and white, red and white and unusual combinations like orange and navy, and green and lilac looked exciting and modern against the background of snow and sun. Adults and children found anoraks, particularly the more conservative styles in plain colours, useful all-purpose winter jackets. People who had no intention of going skiing bought anoraks for everyday wear. They were ideal for the vagaries of the northern climate and were especially suitable for children. Anorak wearing grew in popularity and permanently affected the sales of topcoats to all age groups.

Traditional riding clothes continued to be worn but stretch fabrics began to be used for jodphurs and breeches which retained their shape and were cut without wide wing effects at the sides. Many people rode in casual clothes, anoraks, shirts, sweaters and jeans over or tucked into boots. Traditional leather riding boots with their specialised make had become very expensive. Long rubber boots shaped like a riding boot became a popular alternative style.

Tennis and day dresses were the same length for the first time since the twenties and the easy shift was a very suitable line for active sports. A simple white mini dress was often used for day or tennis wear.

Magazines showed one-piece swimsuits praising their style and line. However, sunbathing had become more popular than ever and most young women wore very brief bikinis. There was an almost limitless selection of prints, stripes and plain colours. Crocheted sets were a popular new style. By the end of the decade it was not possible for bikinis to get any smaller and actually cover anything. Women in the South of France moved on to the next stage and left the tops off for swimming and sunbathing. Soon other parts of the world began to accept topless sunbathing.

The popularity of water sports, scuba diving and surfing introduced one-piece rubber wetsuits. Surfing became a cult sport and a way of life in America and parts of Europe. Cornwall, with its powerful Atlantic waves and sandy beaches, developed its own clubs and shops selling special surfing equipment.

Long evening dresses with embroidered bodices and fullish skirts were still worn for very formal occasions, but evening wear was usually far more varied. Women wore thigh-length silk shift dresses with bands of glitter embroidery at the neck and hem and gold and silver tights with toning shoes or boots. At the same function sweeping kaftans and hippy inspired fantasy dresses were worn. Other women would choose velvet dandy suits and the really avant garde appeared in original Edwardian, 1920s or 1930s dresses.

Deliberately choosing to wear obviously old clothes, sometimes in poor condition, was a new trend during the late sixties and one older people found hard to appreciate. They associated secondhand clothes with the poor and they couldn't understand their daughters rapturising

The end of the sixties—Autumn 69—saw the maxi coat with the longest day length since 1914.

over a rather moth-eaten pre-war silver fox cape or Granny's faded petticoat unearthed from a trunk in the attic.

Young people found a nostalgic charm in old hand-made clothes. It was part of the reaction against the materialistic society and mass-produced clothes in synthetic fabrics.

Clothes with a not too new or over rich look influenced the younger fashions at the end of the decade. Shops opened selling interesting old clothes from any period up to about 1950. Boutiques became less brash. London's Biba was a successful example of the new approach. The clothes were newly made but they were in rather faded colours; greys, purples and lilacs were popular. Twenties and thirties fabrics such as crepe and jersey were used for soft dressmaker style suits and dresses with draped bodices and gathered sleeves.

Fur coats and jackets made from inexpensive skins like rabbit were called 'fun furs' and were dyed unusual shades like dark green, blue-grey and dull orange.

The Biba shops were dark looking, the clothes hooked onto old coatstands; potted palms and plants were placed in corners and at the bottom of stairs and parts of the shops were decorated with coloured ostrich feathers. Fox furs, feather boas and soft pull-on hats were randomly draped over chairs and tables.

Make-up softened to suit the new fashions. False eyelashes were still popular but eye make-up and lipstick were often tinted with peach colour, browns and greys. Blushers were used to emphasise cheek bones and make young faces look more mysterious and worldly. Hair waved into pre-Raphaelite curls or was permed and blow-dried into huge curly 'freak-outs'.

By the end of the sixties a less set approach to following fashion had become established. The Paris couturiers' collections were still publicised in the newspapers and magazines but the designers no longer led the fashion. The best of the ready-to-wear designers in France, Italy and England set the more conventional new lines. France's Yves St. Laurent was one of the most successful. He opened elegant shops with specially designed interiors stocking his exclusive ranges of men's and women's clothes and accessories. St. Laurent's Rive Gauche shops opened in many major cities in Europe and America.

Individual boutiques with their fantasy and nostalgia clothes catered for less conventional customers. Mass-produced clothes were copies from many different sources and buyers and merchandisers presented well edited new trends every few months at prices that most young people could afford.

The sixties slipped away quietly. There was no new war or sudden economic collapse to face but there was a feeling a little like the mood at the end of the twenties that perhaps the party was nearly over, and that the future might not be as easy or as enjoyable. Fashion had become less positive again. Nostalgia for the past seemed more interesting than pushing ahead with dynamic new ideas.

Ankle-and floor-length maxi coats which had been a fringe fashion for two or three years suddenly took on in the autumn and winter of 1969. Girls who had worn the shortest skirts in recorded history now wore the longest since 1914.

At the end of the year the important ready-to-wear designers showed their styles for the following spring and summer. There were still a few maxi and mini skirts but most of the new styles were mid-calf length and older and more severe looking than anything known in the freewheeling sixties which had gone to extremes in length and shapes.

The new styles looked decidedly moderate and middle-of-the-road. They were one of the most serious and damaging flops ever known to the wholesale clothing industry, particularly in America where the mini had taken on later than in Europe. The new fashion was a few years ahead of its time but it foreshadowed the way styling would develop in the more 'serious seventies'.

The 1970s

Unlike some of the earlier decades there was no dramatic change to mark the end of the sixties and the start of the seventies. Although the mood and excitement of the 'Swinging Sixties' was over, life in the early years of the new decade, if not swinging, at least swayed gently. High standards of living, expanding economies and the prosperous consumer societies were still firmly established in the developed countries of the world and many people thought permanently so.

The lack of any positive change was one but not the only reason why the new fashions of 1970 got off to such a bad start. Women's greater self-confidence and independent attitudes together with the power of the mass market were equally important.

The calf-length 'Midi' had been added to the basic silhouette of the late sixties and was shown with familiar styles of shoes, boots and other accessories. Adding length without introducing new lines and altered proportions didn't have enough impact to make women want to buy the longer clothes. The American press dubbed the 'Midi' 'instant age'. Many women agreed and happily carried on wearing minis. Distraught clothing manufacturers were left with considerable stocks of unsold calf-length garments. The season was so disastrous that some firms couldn't carry the losses and went out of business.

It was a severe object lesson for designers, manufacturers and fashion magazines. Something they had long suspected was confirmed; women no longer accepted new designs unless they liked them and felt ready for a change. Fashions had to be suggestions not directives. The clothing industry was made to realise it was the mass market appeal of new styles that determined their success. They had to try and gauge the mood of the general public and get the timing right before launching new ideas. The era of the dictatorial designer which has been waning for ten years was finally over.

Long topcoats were the only garments where the midi had some moderate success. Maxi coats from lower calf to floor length had been a young fashion craze at the end of 1969 and the beginning of 1970, particularly in Britain. The maxi helped to get women used to the idea of a longer coat line and the mid-calf lengths shown for the following autumn sold reasonably well, especially in France and Italy where very long coats had been considered too extreme. Quieter calf-length styles appealed to many continental women who preferred a more understated way of dressing.

With their self-confidence shaken designers and manufacturers faced 1971 with a resolve to give the public whatever it wanted as long as it sold. Variety of choice seemed to be the safest course.

Old favourites, minis and trouser suits, were revived and several new ideas were tried. Front buttoning, top of the calf-length skirts with the buttons left open to the thighs, showing matching or contrasting tightly fitting shorts called hot pants' were introduced. Shorts were also shown with tailored blazer jackets and fancy patterned close fitting knitted tops. The attitude of the fashion world seemed to be, 'If they want to show legs let them wear hot pants'.

Tight shorts needed a very good figure to be shown to advantage. Many women felt that their proportions were not good enough and they were too self-conscious to wear such a revealing style. Girls with the right shape loved hot pants and caused a sensation dancing in their satin disco shorts.

Tailored jackets and loose hip-length coats with heavily padded shoulders worn with knee-

Brash looking young fashions of the early
seventies—satin fabrics shaped to the figure.

'Hot pants' and platform soles became crazes in the
early seventies.

length dresses or skirts formed part of the 'tarty look' and in particular the tarty style of the
1940s. Heavy make-up, loosely piled hair, shoulder bags and platform soled shoes completed
the all too authentic appearance of a brassy looking women during the Second World War. A
deliberately brash style in questionable taste was a far cry from the couture elegance Dior and
Balenciaga had presided over for so many years.

The 'tarty look' was only partly successful. Padded shoulders and knee-length skirts were a
flop but some of the details of the 1940s styles took on. Heavier make-up, lips emphasised
with the use of lip gloss, and Rita Hayworth waves and curls were quite popular. *Diamanté*
jewellery, stars, hair slides and crescent-shaped clips pinned on jackets and dresses were
successful crazes. Satin was widely used for shirts, jackets and trousers. Broad shouldered fox
fur capes and coats, particularly originals from the late thirties, became prize possessions with
the young and were often worn over modern casual clothes, shirts, knitwear and trousers or
jeans tucked into high boots.

The forties influence was seen at its strongest in shoe designs. Platform soles were added to
every kind of men's and women's shoes and boots. Women's shoes with peep toes, sling backs

The
1970s

'Flares' trousers, cut to widen from the knee, was one of the most commercial shapes during the first half of the decade.

and ankle straps had thick high heels or deep wedges. Dyed reptile skins, shiny patent leather and kid in dark or bright colours and sometimes combinations of two or three contrasting shades were all popular. Fashionable footwear was more prominent and extreme than at any other time in this century. Some platform soles were so high they rivalled traditional Chinese and Japanese styles and the built-up soles of the Chopines worn in Europe during the 16th century. A moderate platform sole gave height and could look quite elegant but the extreme designs were heavily disproportionate to the legs and some styles were so ugly that people in other times would have felt sorry for anyone having to wear them as surgical shoes or boots. Despite difficulties in walking, sprained ankles and detrimental remarks from the older generation, these styles sold very successfully during the first half of the seventies.

Many fashion conscious women, bored with the controversy over skirt lengths and not wanting to wear minis, midis, hot pants or dress up in garish 1940s fashions, wore trouser outfits for all occasions. St. Laurent-inspired tailored trouser suits in black wool gaberdine, neat mannish stripes or checked suitings, were worn with smart town accessories, a classic below the knee-length raincoat and round owlish looking sunglasses. It became one of the most popular international fashions worn by stylish young women.

Knitted outfits comprising body-shaped sweaters in plains or fancy patterns, long cardigans, rib knitted trousers and matching hats and long scarves in wool or synthetic and wool mixtures were popular styles with a wide age group.

Feminine evening trousers and tops were made in printed silks, patterned jersey or flowing black or pastel coloured crepes. They had full sleeved blouse or tunic tops, usually worn over the trousers loose, or lightly belted round the high hip line with a cord or a self-fabric belt fastened with an ornate jewelled or metal clasp. Trousers were very wide and often looked like a long flared skirt until women moved. They were usually worn with high or wedge-heeled evening sandals.

Fashionable trousers were all cut wide and full round the hem. The two popular styles were 'flares' and 'bags'. Flares cut as tightly as ever over the seat and thighs, widened from below the knees into bell-bottomed fullness. Men and women wore them over fairly high-heeled boots and shoes with lifted soles which gave the leg an elongated look from the knee downwards.

'Bags' were inspired by the loose-legged trousers with front pleats worn in the twenties and thirties. The seventies versions fitted much more closely over the seat and because they were worn over built up shoes or boots they looked leggier and more elegant than the droopier pre Second World War styles. Quite a lot of fashion conscious young women and men wore the

The elegant Saint Laurent style of trouser suit became popular with many women.

'Unisex' was a term derived from the trend for sexes to dress alike.

looser cut as a dressier alternative trouser, but many people felt it was a harder to wear and less flattering style than the flared line. Baggier trousers with varying leg widths remained fashionable for ten years and although reasonably popular they were never as universally worn as some of the other more commercial trouser shapes of the decade.

Hair styles, like other areas of fashion, were more varied. Women were less conformist about adopting obviously fashionable hair-dos; choosing a cut that was generally contemporary but particularly suited to the individual was a further reflection of women's more self-confident attitude over their appearance.

High contrived looking hair was considered very out of date by the early seventies. Many women, however, used to raised fullness, still liked some blow dried lift. Permed curls in halo shaped 'freak outs' or shoulder hanging waves or ringlets were also still popular. Well known hairdressers devised styles based on skilful and imaginative new shapes. They gained a following for their designs and other hair stylists produced versions of the most succesful new shapes.

Young men's fashions at their most dandified stage in the early seventies—long hair, body-fitting velvet clothes, high boots.

The curly hairstyle, as worn by David Essex, was popular throughout the decade.

A layered effect, slightly raised but following the crown in soft feathery waves, brushed together at the back of the neck and short enough to clear collars, became extremely popular for all ages. A similar style, especially liked and worn by young women and men, was the 'Onion Cut'. Layered hair followed the line of the crown, shaped into the nape of the neck and then straggled out onto the shoulders in rather wispy points or curls. Updated versions of the long bobs of the thirties and forties were re-introduced. They were cut to turn under softly round the face and onto the shoulders, giving a fuller and less set appearance compared to the styles of the earlier decades.

Hair care became much more important. Women began to take at least as much trouble over the condition of their hair as the way it was styled. Trichologists were consulted by many more women and men and regular treatments at trichology clinics were undertaken by a growing number of people. Healthy looking hair, well cut and shaped but generally worn in a natural uncontrived form became the way many young people wanted their hair to look.

During the early seventies fashions in hair styles, colours, materials, lines of clothes and footwear designs, applied more and more to both women, men and children. 'Unisex' had been used since the mid-sixties to describe the trend for the sexes to dress alike. By the seventies fashion was nearer to a unisex style than at any other time in this century. Adults and children often had the same hair style cut by the same hairdresser. Fashionably cut hair made a tremendous improvement to the appearance of many children.

The designs and shapes of the contemporary garments were very suitable for children. Many styles were scaled down to children's sizes. Miniature versions of women's knitted trouser outfits with matching scarves and hats were worn by boys and girls under school age. Conventional uniforms or clothes were still worn in many schools but fashion conscious children often gave them an up-to-date look. Boys in grey flannel suits, white shirts and school ties had trendy long hair, and boots with high wooden heels and platform soles under their trousers although not approved of were often worn. Many girls got away with wearing a variety of very modern hair styles and like the boys whenever possible clumped about in

By the seventies jeans had become a way of life and most people under forty possessed at least one pair.

fashionably heavy shoes and boots. For out of school hours the selection of children's clothes was almost as great as the range of teenage and young adult fashions. The children's market was growing in importance. Parents were more willing to buy the fast changing styles in children's clothes than many of the earlier generations would have been.

Children were very fashion conscious and had definite ideas on what they liked. Proofed anorak-type jackets and leather or leather-look fabrics with sheepskin or fur fabric linings used for narrow fitting flying jackets replaced classic topcoats and raincoats in many children's wardrobes. Trousers or bib-fronted dungarees with flared hems in brightly coloured corduroy or blue denim and sometimes teamed with matching blouson jackets with zip fronts and pockets were popular with children and teenagers. For parties boys often wore fitted shirts in textured fabrics or prints, soft floaty scarves, and flared velvet trousers with wide belts fastened with fancy buckles.

Young men's fashions reached the most dandified stage of the century. Hair was as varied in cut and length as the women's styles and sometimes dressed identically. Trailing cavalier curls and neatly turned under page-boy bobs sat on the shoulders of tailored business suits,

Ranges of denim garments catered for the whole family.

Rubber-soled denim shoe, designed to go with jeans.

Children followed the trend and wore the same style denim dungarees, jeans and accessories.

tough leather jackets and casual clothes. It was not unusual to see burly motorcyclists or men working on building sites with loose flowing locks or their long hair tied back in ponytails.

Fashion conscious men sometimes required as many visits to the hairdressers as their girlfriends. Tinting and colouring had become more acceptable and perming had also become increasingly popular with various styles of all-over curls.

Facial hair, long sideburns, moustaches and beards had been fashionable from the mid-sixties onwards. They became even more so during the first half of the seventies. Some men in quite conservative occupations presented a surprisingly hairy appearance with long hair styles, heavy drooped Mexican bandit moustaches and shaped beards. Such theatrical hairiness would not have been permissible in conventional jobs ten years before. Even men in the artistic world would have been considered eccentric. The biblical looking heads of many young men in the early seventies were rather incongruous with the colourful body fitted clothes of the time. Large-collared shirts in mauves, pinks and blues, plain or printed, were darted front and back to shape the figure and unless the man was slim to the point of skinniness they tended to look undersized. Even the suspicion of a rounded stomach showed all too clearly. Shirts were worn with wide 'kipper ties' or left open at the neck and down the front to show flimsy scarves loosely tied or a variety of necklaces and crosses. Other kinds of costume jewellery were also quite popular, small gold gipsy-style earrings, bracelets, some with the wearers' name engraved on disks, and quite ornate rings sometimes worn several at a time on the fingers of each hand.

Jackets, topcoats and raincoats with wide revers were shaped to the body. They had high armholes and narrow sleeves. Overcoats were often calf-length midis. Old military greatcoats were a craze with the young and to add period costume swagger style-conscious young men tucked jeans or velvet trousers into high leather boots. Velvet was as popular as ever and some men wore them as everyday garments. Silk braided velvet jackets were worn with casual open-necked shirts and flared jeans.

The difference in the clothes worn by the younger and older generation was very noticeable. Most older men wisely realised the flambuoyant styles were not suitable for them, although some of the new young styles were gradually adopted by all age groups. Velvet jackets and suits replaced barathea dinner jackets in many wardrobes. It was a less obviously formal style but it looked equally right for a dinner party, a reception or a ball. Jeans were also now worn by many more people and age groups. Blue denim jeans were the most universally worn garments of the century and the nearest men, women and children have got to wearing a uniform. Jeans had been worn by men as working pants in America since the middle of the last century. During the 1940s teenagers in the States started to wear them for their everyday life. In the fifties they became popular in many more countries and in keeping with the fashionable curvy body fit of the time they were worn tight enough to show the shape of the seat and thighs. The popularity of jeans spread quickly in the sixties. Children lived in jeans; they were practical and modern. Teenagers and young adults wore them as tight as possible to provocatively show off their figures. Style conscious men and women in their thirties and forties also started wearing jeans. In a decade when youth, or at least a youthful image, was so important the not-so-young felt jean wearing allied them to the active modern world.

By the seventies jeans had become a way of life and there were few people under forty in

Mid-seventies fashion jeans were narrow and straight cut in the leg and were often worn with bold tartan jackets.

America, Europe and many other parts of the world who didn't possess at least one pair. Apart from school uniforms and special occasions, children and teenagers habitually wore jeans. The anti-Establishment and anti-fashion young wore them deliberately shabby with ragged fringed hems over unclean scuffed gym shoes. Jeans in better condition but not too new looking were worn with wide leather belts and over or tucked into Western boots as part of the ever popular style of the later 20th-century for an urban cowboy look.

Neat jeans with well known designer and brand names were worn by a wider than ever age group of style conscious men and women. Well made-up, fashionably hairstyled women in expensive jackets, fur coats, blouses and knitwear, substituted jeans instead of a tailored skirt or trousers and wore them with elegant boots. Trendy moustached men wore jeans with tight leather jackets, sharply cut blazers or modernised cotton safari tunics.

Denim and the jean influence developed into other kinds of garments. Dungarees and boiler suits became popular alternatives, especially for women and children. Shorts with jean styling took on with children and young adults and denim type fabrics with jean stitching were used for bikinis and men's swimming trunks. Hats, caps, belts, shoes and boots were also made in denim and to add some colour and variety they were sometimes decorated with studs or embroidered with brightly coloured flowers.

Jeans and denim garments had become the mass selling clothes of the age. Denim was made into raincoats, fur fabric lined topcoats and jackets, long and short skirts, jodphurs and

Army caps and badges teamed up with blue jeans.

The unisex 'Army look' became popular, with garments decorated with military insignia.

The brutal looking cult style of the skinheads developed in contrast to the men's dandified fashions of the early seventies.

ski pants. Denim dresses were edged with frills and ribbons; the fabric was used for every conceivable kind of garment but none rivalled the ever growing number of jeans. Special jeans shops opened, departmental stores had jeans sections and no young men's or women's shop was without a selection of well known makes.

The perfect fitting jean was a quest with many people; the merits of different brands were endlessly debated; loyalty to certain names was professed and people happily advertised the makers' names across their seats. Jeans are functional, almost classless, and until something better is invented, although their popularity may wane from time to time, are unlikely to go out of fashion.

T-shirts, like jeans, started life as basic workwear. They complemented one another and their growth in popularity has followed the same time span. Although T-shirts have always been a simple slip-over shape, by the seventies their types varied from cheap vest-like tops to fancy stripes, USA university styles with names, slogans and messages, and top of the market boutique and couture designs in silky knits embroidered with gold thread and glitter motifs.

In the first half of the seventies the Vietnam war had produced strong anti-war reactions amongst some of the young generation. In contradiction to the anti-war sentiments, army looking clothes became a very commercial young fashion fad. Few people relished the idea of war but they wanted to wear military looking clothes with fashionable hairstyles and accessories. The glamour of wearing uniforms was liked but not the unpleasant realities of fighting a real war. Young men and women wore khaki or camourflaged US style caps overs their long wavy hair. Military shirts with fake or original badges and stripes on the sleeves were worn with necklaces or fancy scarves. Tight khaki jeans, shorts or authentic combat trousers were teamed with gym shoes or leather fashion boots.

Trendy commercialised fashions were not admired by all the younger generation. In Britain a new rather brutal looking cult style developed. Some working class boys, in stark contrast to long wavy curls, cropped their hair very short. They wore plain vest-like tops or dull looking shirts and sleeveless pullovers with baggy-seated trousers or jeans, often hitched up high with braces worn over shirts or tops. The trousers were turned up above the ankle to show heavy laced working boots known as 'bovver boots'. Boys wearing the style were called 'skinheads', 'boot boys' or 'bovver boys'. There was a lot of unfavourable publicity over the new cult. It was associated with mindless aggression. Skinheads were reputed to be full of 'aggro' and looking for trouble. Many young men simply liked to identify with the tough macho style but had no intention of getting involved in hooliganism.

Higher class, style conscious young men, anxious to spot a new trend and remembering the influence beatnicks and hippies had on fashion, decided the time had arrived for short hair. Fashionable hair stylists started to cut a neat all-over length. Although short by the accepted standards, it was more flattering and fuller at the sides and back than the old pre-war 'short back and sides' and nothing like as shorn as the skinheads' crop. Although shorter hair for men was declared fashionable, only the advanced few had it cut. Most men were not ready to give up their long styles.

The careless effect clothes, selling in large quantities, were comparatively easy to make and didn't require too exacting standards of quality. To sell into a highly competitive market wholesalers and retailers looked for ways of cutting costs. Getting clothes made in countries with cheaper labour provided the answer. Manufacturing in India and the Far East had been growing since the early sixties but with the ultra casual clothes of the seventies it developed rapidly. Soon it was not only the cheaper end of the clothing market that bought from the developing countries. Designers and merchandisers from well known brand names in Europe and America also developed prototypes and arranged for bulk production in Hong Kong and other countries in the East. Although still assured a place, because of production costs making clothes in the traditional clothing centres sadly began to decline.

As a reaction to mass-produced jeans and the army look, many women began to want to wear something more feminine, a complete contrast, a soft frilly alternative to tough mannish styles. Wales's Laura Ashley who had been developing a following for her country style, captured the reactionary mood and became internationally known. Her Victorian prints, particularly her small flower designs, on soft colours or dark backgrounds were used for blouses and dresses trimmed with lace, broderie anglaise and ribbons. Bodices were tucked and pleated and ankle-length skirts were lightly gathered into the waistline.

Long romantic dresses and skirts were not practical for the rush and bustle of everyday life in the later 20th-century, but the Laura Ashley type of outfit made charming occasion clothes for young mothers and daughters. Brides and bridesmaids were often in Laura Ashley style dresses. Many women loved changing out of their masculine trouser suits into delicate long dresses or skirts.

Laura Ashley's curtains and wallpapers were at least as well known as her clothing designs. A gentler, more natural style was very appealing. After 30 years of expansion and growing materialism people began to question where it was leading and how long it would be before the world's natural resources started to run out. Conservation, simple country styles in food, interior decoration and clothes, were all part of the new attitude.

The film and pop world continued to have an influence on the way young people looked and dressed. It was, however, a more general influence. Although there were many successful new stars in the seventies, they tended to exaggerate or endorse current fashions rather than start completely new styles.

Elton John was famous for his very high heels and clog like soles. He made his shoe styles a gimmick not to be taken too seriously. David Bowie was one of the most style conscious singers and actors. He wore many of the most extreme men's fashions of the decade. The successful girl singer Debbie Harry, of Blondie, was one of the first to wear the revived mini-skirt.

The glamorous looks of the young women in the popular television series 'Charlie's Angels', particularly Farrah Fawcett-Major, epitomised the healthy, well-groomed Californian style with natural looking make-up and flattering casual hair cuts softly framing the face and shoulders. Charlie's Angels' looks were widely copied by many women in their twenties and thirties. It was a youthful and yet mature style that many women, especially in America, felt they could identify with.

The Middle East war in the autumn of 1973 was a watershed for many countries. Until the war started a boom was in progress. It was to be the last one of its kind for the rest of the decade. Within six months fuel prices had risen alarmingly, inflation was growing quickly and world trade had gone into recession. A more serious period had started and fashion, as always, was right on cue. Longer skirts and heavier looking styles had already arrived. The timing was right and they began to take on.

Laura Ashley's Victorian prints and feminine clothes were a welcome alternative.

Farrah Fawcett-Majors epitomised the healthy Californian style.

Kenzo, the clever young Japanese designer whose Paris ready-to-wear clothes were labelled Jap, did much to bring in the new fashion. As early as 1973 he was showing longer gathered or flared skirts and dresses. Mandy Clapperton, one of English *Vogue*'s bright fashion editors, was one of the first to wear his new line, dressed in a blue needlecord skirt with a wide waistband and flared fullness to a calf-length hem, almost identical to the styles that had been worn by girls in the fifties.

Fashions for summer 1974 were longer and more mature looking. Shorter, neater permed hair was introduced. Head-fitting hats with shallow dipping brims, similar to the styles of the early thirties, were quite popular. Many dresses had shirt bodices and pleated or softly flared skirts. Shoes were more delicate with higher slimmer heels. There was a nostalgia for the twenties and thirties. The popular film *The Great Gatsby* helped to promote a nostalgic mood.

The autumn fashions confirmed the trend for longer, heavier looking outfits started by Kenzo a year earlier. Hair was covered by pull-on felt or knitted hats. Fuller cut blouses were topped with pullovers and knitted waistcoats. Loose hip-length jackets were added. Mid or lower calf-length skirts in heavyish wollens were gathered into the waist, the various garments were covered by a long swirling cape or a roomy hooded topcoat, one or two long scarves, knitted gloves or mittens and long squashy legged boots called 'baggy boots'. The outfits were aptly called 'the layered look'. It was an older style that tended to make even the slimmest

The 1970s

Winter 1974: fashion registers the chillier economic climate with the 'layered look'.

women look pounds heavier and gave some the appearance of a prosperous pre-revolutionary peasant.

During the next two years layered clothes with strong peasant influences continued. They were sometimes called 'ethnic' clothes. As an alternative to long boots showing under skirts, baggy trousers were worn, making another layer and turning the dress or skirt into an over-tunic. The inevitable boots were worn under the trousers and to add yet more layers thick woollen socks or leg warmers, with fancy Peruvian style patternings, were pulled over the trouser legs.

The more extreme high fashion styles were not widely worn but a peasant influence with longer skirts and various interchangeable layered tops and accessories which could be easily made by the home dressmaker and knitter took on with many women who found they could devise their own versions adapted to their way of life and provide a practical alternative to jean wearing.

Fashion had once again completely changed in ten years. The fashionable woman of the mid-sixties wore clothes of childlike simplicity, brief and undersized. The fashion conscious woman of the mid-seventies wore everything big and baggy. The idea of contrived bagginess would have seemed ludicrous to women of the previous decade.

Gradually eroding living standards caused by inflation, the prominence of organised labour and a swing towards left-wing domination in many countries helped popularise workwear clothes for men and women. Societies have always tended to copy the clothes worn by their most powerful members. In earlier centuries court circles dominated; later, the landed gentry, and at the beginning of the 20th century, the prosperous middle classes were at their

The
1970s

Peasant styles were still an important influence in
1976 and were often called 'ethnic' clothes.

Colourful layers and boots help to keep women warm
in the mid-seventies.

Practical jackets like this hooded duffle coat were inspired by workwear garments.

most influential. By the mid-seventies the workers were showing power and strength and their style of clothes was copied by manufacturers as fashion garments for the mass market. Overalls and dungarees had been a fringe fashion since the sixties but during the later seventies they became basic everyday garments and although not as widely worn as jeans they were extremely popular.

Style conscious firms produced slick, well fitting boiler suits in a variety of fabrics; for the summer they were made in bright and pastel coloured cottons; clear pinks, light blues were used. Some girls started to wear them for evening occasions as well as practical day clothes. They were accessorised with jewellery and high-heeled sandals for parties and dances. Trousered garments were especially suitable for the athletic movements of accomplished disco-dancing.

Bib-fronted dungarees were also worn by young men and women as practical and fashion garments. Corduroy, denim and beige or khaki cotton twills were used for everyday styles; white cotton dungarees over colourful T-shirts for parties and summer holidays.

Trouser shapes altered in the second half of the decade. Narrow legged styles replaced flares as the most popular basic cut. They were not as tight and narrow in the leg as the styles worn in the late fifties and early sixties but the slimmer, straighter line was flattering and the narrow cut looked a better proportion with boiler suits and dungarees.

Anoraks had become popular all-purpose autumn and winter jackets. They suited the practical trouser outfits and universally worn jeans. With the influence of working clothes designers smartened up the styling of zip-fronted or press-stud fastening padded jackets, the cut was improved and fashionable details such as shoulder epaulettes and shaped bands round the neckline instead of collars were added. They were made in fashionable colours — wine, creamy beiges and army greens. To fit in with the big looking jackets, knitwear shapes changed. The new silhouette for casual wear was bulky at the top and narrow in the legs. Skinny fitting pullovers and cardigans didn't suit the new line. Loose

Padded jackets, roomy sweaters and straight cut cord jeans became popular in country looking casual clothes.

'Punk' fashions started as a lower class cult fashion, spiky hair cuts, startling colours and footless tights.

sweaters in fancy stitches, patternings, or in the plain colours of the season were more suited to the roomy jacket designs, narrow cord jeans and boots. It became one of the most popular casual methods of dress for young men and women.

Interlined tunics in quilted, proofed fabrics, usually in khaki, had originally been designed to add extra warmth to working outfits. They became all-purpose garments for town and country wear. In Britain the middle and upper classes took the style up and gave it county association, it became part of a recognisable set of clothes. Women wore their quilted 'huskies' over high quality knitwear, shirts and check pleated skirts. Dark tights, stacked heel shoes decorated with clips or chains, a leather shoulder bag and an expensive looking head-scarf tied on, not under, the chin, completed what English *Harper's Bazaar* christened 'The Sloane Ranger Look' epitomising a style most frequently seen in London's fashionable Sloane Street.

A new lower class cult fashion developed during the later seventies. Hair was cut short and spiky all over or cropped at the sides with a high standing tuft of hair running from front to back over the head like a North American Indian. Hair was dyed startling colours, bright pink or green, sometimes several strong colours were used on the same head to give striped and patched effects. Faces were pale with highlights of colour on the cheeks and round the eyes. The area round just one eye was sometimes made up in multi-coloured geometric shapes. Some of the more outrageous had safety pins through their noses or ears. Clothes were usually in black or strong colours with black, particularly pink; ocelot prints and bright red Royal Stuart tartans were also teamed with black.

Loose T-shirts had messages, slogans or ink-like blobs printed on them. Jackets and trousers were in matt or sheen cotton and occasionally in leather or leather-looking fabrics. They were decorated with zips and straps. Trousers called 'bondage trousers' were joined together at the back with loose dangling straps; lengths finished well above the ankle to show bright socks and high laced rubber or leather combat boots. The new style was called 'Punk' and the wearers 'Punk Rockers'. Both sexes wore similar outfits but the girls sometimes wore mini-skirts with brightly coloured footless tights and pointed toed stiletto heeled court shoes or ankle boots.

Few styles have been so loudly condemned. To many people Punk fashions were deliberately ugly and made the wearer unnecessarily unattractive. New fashions are always

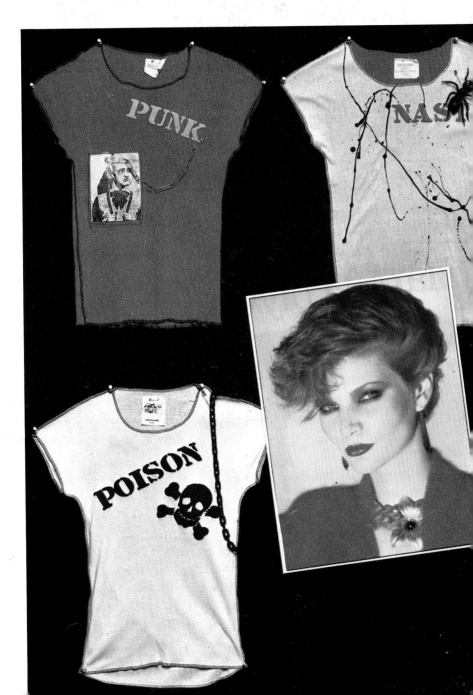

Special punk designs were used for
T-shirts, and (*inset*) the
punk style was refined and adapted
for a higher class market.

overstated and the younger generation often want to shock and outrage their elders with wildly unconventional clothes. For those in older age groups it was certainly difficult to understand the appeal of Punk styles. However, during the next few years fashion designers refined and adapted some of the new designs and many of the accepted fashions at the end of the seventies were Punk inspired.

During the second half of the seventies the style conscious generation, young in the late fifties and sixties, approached middle-age; they belonged to an age group who had considered a youthful image very important. Many of the more affluent members of this generation made efforts to keep young and fashion helped. Women growing up in the fifties had often looked older than their years. With the little girl styles of the sixties they managed to look much younger. In the mid and late seventies the more mature looking expensive clothes enabled them to present a glamorous, youngish appearance without having to wear clothes that would by then have been obviously too young. Hair care, exercises and diet were practised regularly. Men in the same age group also worked at their appearance and watched their diet. A slimmish figure, modern hair-styling and flattering casual clothes helped many men to look comparatively young.

Active sports were an important part of keeping fit. Both sexes took up jogging. Special colourful and practical jogging outfits were adopted, either a pullover top and trousers or all-in-one track suits. Jogging outfits were comfortable and easy; people started to wear them as general casual outfits. Some women dressed their velour jogging clothes up with stylish accessories and wore them as informal evening wear.

The 1970s was a very sports conscious decade. Active sports clothes improved and developed. Many more well-stocked sports shops opened and large stores gave extra floor space for exciting sports departments. Knitted tennis shirts and shorts in easy-care fabrics, braided or edged in contrasting colours, navy, reds and greens on white gave tennis outfits a smart co-ordinated appearance. The famous tennis player, Björn Borg, popularised the wearing of a plain coloured or striped band across the forehead and round the skull to keep long hair off the face. Suzanne Lenglen, the well known French women's player of the twenties, had introduced women's headbands for the same reason.

Sailing clothes combined practicability with colourful styling. Shiny weatherproof jackets with adjustable drawstrings to close hoods round the neck and face and to tighten wrists and hems, were used on two and three colour sailing jackets with zip fronts and pockets. Plain and striped knitwear and towelling tops were designed in nautical looking navy and white; sailing themes were further emphasised with the use of embroidered or embossed ship's wheels and anchors. Fashionable looking footwear had functional details. Moccasin deck shoes were made with special rubber gripping soles. Sailing wellingtons in navy or bright yellow were designed with practical cords slotted round the top to close the boots onto the legs in rough weather.

Ski clothes developed a definite space-age look. Padded anoraks and trousers or all-in-one ski suits were made in white, metallic silver or bright colours with a metallic finish. Boots with their impressive modernistic shapes and fastenings were called 'Moon Boots'. An expensive modern ski outfit certainly had an astronaut look. For after-ski wear, huge caveman type boots in fur fabric with non-slip soles, were popular in fashionable resorts.

Shooting and riding clothes have changed the least over the decades. There have been

Classic suits were still worn and hair was not noticeably long or short.

Fashion interest in men's casual clothes developed strongly. Blouson jackets, check shirts and cord jeans were very popular.

slight alternations in cut and less set outfits have gradually become more acceptable but the correct clothes for the sports have remained surprisingly unaltered. Deer stalkers, tweed Norfolk jackets, knickerbockers, long woollen socks and laced ankle boots, very similar to the styles of the 1900s were still worn in the seventies. Younger men, however, often preferred proofed army style jackets with hoods and plenty of useful pockets, worn with trousers or jeans tucked into khaki green wellingtons.

Classic made-to-measure riding clothes, unbeatable for style and elegance, became almost prohibitively expensive. They were still worn for all competitive riding events and usually for hunting, but for informal hacking everyday casual wear styles, already popular alternatives in the sixties, became even more generally worn.

In 1977 and 1978 designers slimmed down the rather over-loaded silhouette and tried to revive more definite shapes and lines with very wide shoulders, slimmer body fittings and slightly shorter skirts. New lines were a mixture of the clothes in spage-age fiction, the 1940s and the 1950s. Enormously wide winged or rounded shoulders, like American footballers', heavily padded, did not take on; like the 'midi' at the beginning of the decade, women simply turned down a style they didn't like and manufacturers were left with stocks of unsaleable garments. Unstructured versions of the mannish jackets of the forties with fairly broad shoulders were reasonably successful. They were worn with silky blouses, T-shirts, jeans or tight slit skirts reminiscent of the fifties. Soft, slim-looking wrap-over dresses in jersey or silk type materials in plain colours and prints were popular with women. The lighter styles were worn with more delicate shoes with oval toes and thinner heels; ankle boots and townier versions of cowboy boots with finer toes and heels also became quite popular.

Softer adaptations of the rolled-up hairstyles of the late thirties and early forties introduced to complement the more sophisticated clothes were worn by some women, usually for dressed up occasions.

Although an unlayered silhouette was a welcome progression, women made it clear that hard defined shapes and lines with precise styling were not wanted. Designers and manufacturers had to be careful not to try and over-reach their influence and direct fashion into difficult, angular looking silhouettes.

Inflation had made good quality clothes so expensive, even well off women bought with the investment value of new garments in mind. Classic raincoats, separates and accessories, were chosen because they would be useful and the styling slow to date. Class distinction through dress showed more clearly amongst mature women than at any time since the early fifties; many families, faced with constantly strained budgets, couldn't afford the spiralling cost of good quality clothes. For those who could, safe classic styling, although elegant, looked older and perhaps rather dull compared to many of the fashions of the previous 15 years.

London in the late seventies was very different from its swinging image of the mid-sixties.

Jogging was part of the craze for keeping fit and outfits developed for this gradually began to be worn as casual wear.

By 1977 designers had slimmed down the silhouette and showed a lighter more delicate style for summer clothes.

Britain had been more adversely affected by industrial problems and inflation than many other countries; visitors from abroad noticed with regret the changes. The inexpensive, clever type of young fashions London had been famed for in the sixties were less evident. Many people were having to make do with shabby clothes and lowering standards of living. The scope for experimental designing that had once flourished was now more limited. However, some of Britain's established designers, despite the difficult circumstances, carried on producing flattering clothes in unusual and inventive designs and fabrics. Names like Zandra Rhodes, Janice Wainwright, Jean Muir and Bill Gibb were still internationally known for their unique special occasion clothes.

Italy was also experiencing considerable problems but they were less noticeable than the ones in Britain, and Italian ready-to-wear clothes more than held their own in the international market. Italian designers didn't try and promote controversial new silhouettes for women's clothes; their exceptionally good colour sense combined with the imaginative use of fabrics and styling produced desirable easy to wear clothes.

Italian knitwear was well known for its inventiveness. Missoni produced some of the most artistic combinations of yarns, stitches and colours. Their designs were sold in many countries all over the world.

Most of the new styles in shoes and boots originated in Italy. Different designs and shapes were introduced regularly and although catering for a wide age group and price range Italian designs were usually tasteful and well proportioned.

Leather and suede had been used for fashion garments since the fifties but, apart from jackets and coats, its popularity had been limited. During the later seventies Italian designers promoted the use of supple leathers and suedes in a wide range of colours from delicate pastel shades to rich autumnal reds, greens and browns. Some of the skins were printed or embroidered and used for feminine blouses and dresses as well as the casual kind of clothes more usually associated with leather or suede. Although expensive, women found them very appealing and a permanent section of the fashion market became established for suede and leather which developed and changed like other areas of fashion each season.

Italy had been an important influence on men's clothes for several decades. Its influence became even stronger during the late seventies. Designers like Giorgio Armani set new silhouettes in men's clothes with considerable authority. Although his designs were not presented in the dictatorial way the women's couturiers had once enjoyed; his shapes and styles did influence the direction in men's fashions.

Skinny fit and long hair were completely out of date by the end of the decade. They had been replaced by shorter hair, and a broader, bulkier, more masculine but still very fashion conscious style. Cropped hair had been tried by some men but the most popular lengths were not noticeably long or short; well shaped hair, cut to suit the individual, predominated. Neat beards and moustaches were still worn but there was a swing away from facial hair and back to a clean-shaven appearance.

Broad padded shoulders were promoted for men as well as women and were nearly as unsuccessful. Shoulder emphasis rather than padding appealed to many younger men; rows of stitching on an extended shoulder line or a hooded or capped effect at the shoulders were popular for casual jackets in leather or wool. Shirt styles changed; large collars were replaced by small ones and tight body fit with bagginess. The intentionally loose fit was described as the new 'baggy look' for shirts. Ties were small and narrow, similar to the styles of the late fifties. Scarves and costume jewellery were less popular. Pullovers, like shirts, were roomy and oversized. Fashion conscious men who at the beginning of the decade squeezed themselves into a size too small, now bought knitwear deliberately large.

Raincoats were military looking with wide, loose shoulders and full cut body shapes decorated with army style pockets and shoulder tabs; khaki greens and dull beiges emphasised the tough functional look. Classic, straight-cut cord or denim jeans were the most popular trousers. The more fashion conscious styles were loose around the thighs and tapered at the ankles. Footwear varied from lightweight running shoes and moccasins to strapped or laced ankle boots and pull-on calf length cowboy styles usually worn under trousers.

Stylish leather clothes were as popular for men as they were for women and there was a wide variety of casual blouson style jackets, waistcoats and trousers. Hip-length leather coats with padded linings or wadded interlinings were smart and practical for the winter. Young men now rarely wore tailored overcoats. Anoraks and padded jackets were far more popular. Leather clothes were much admired but too expensive for many people.

Fashion interest in men's clothes during the decade had shifted almost completely into casual clothes. Although many men still wore conventional suits, ties, shirts and shoes in their daily business life, all age groups enjoyed changing into more informal clothes, and a growing number of men wore Italian inspired casual outfits for most occasions, business or leisure.

America's well respected professional designers produced contemporary clothes with the latest international fashion trends for their home market and export. Some of the designers were well known outside the States but their collections were not followed with the same interest as the French and Italian designers. America's influence on fashion was through their

Left: 1979 introduced slimmer body shapes and shorter skirts. *Right:* Saint Laurent outfit, spring 1979, showing the new silhouette with wider shoulders.

advanced living styles; well equipped homes and several cars per family had done much to bring casual wear to the forefront of fashion. Western clothes, teenage cult fashions and sports clothes, especially the new water sports and jogging, had often originated in America. Health diets, beauty care including new cosmetics and hair styling and conditioning, were also pioneered by the Americans. Their influences were on modern ways of looking and dressing, geared to technical and social changes. It was a practical approach, the functional aspect was worked out. Style, colour and fabric details were then added. The Americans called it 'real life clothes' and Europeans copied the new approach, often without realisisng it. Jeans, T-shirts and jogging outfits were just a few examples of 'real life' garments adopted all over the world.

The harder realities of life in the late seventies reinforced the popularity of useful and practical clothes. Fashion magazines emphasised the versatility of garments and praised them for their plain lines. Details were gone into, pointing out why a garment was a good buy, its useful colour, the quality of the material and the importance of a style that would not date.

Attitudes had changed fundamentally. In the late sixties the newness of a style, how trendy it was, the fantasy appeal of wearing strong fashion, had been the noteworthy points emphasised in the glossy magazines.

American designers were particularly good at giving the more functional clothes some extra flair. They perfected the cut of their jeans; the right boots and belts were designed to complement any slight changes in waistlines or leg widths. Women's all-purpose jackets were masculine without being hard and dowdy. Cleverly-styled blouses and knitwear, well marketed, were displayed near the jackets, trousers and skirts they were designed to go with. Colour and texture themes were promoted each season.

Fashion changes in 1979 concentrated on changes of detail rather than costly new lines. Spiky hair cuts, bright colours, shorter skirts, pointed-toed stiletto-heeled shoes, all combined to give an inexpensive mixture of designer refined Punk styles and a revival of the mid-sixties. Just as the younger generation in the late forties had hankered nostalgically for the last fun period, the twenties, teenagers at the end of the seventies, worried by growing unemployment and worsening international relations, took refuge in the most recent light-hearted decade, the sixties.

Designers, particularly the leading French ready-to-wear designers like Kenzo, had tried to promote the return of the mini for a couple of years. A few advanced young women had worn the new mini, usually as an elongated sweater with boots, and skirt lengths had gradually inched up from the middle to the top of the calf. By the end of 1979 many more teenage girls started to enjoy wearing minis as an extra style. They often had flowing dresses and skirts with below the knee length hemlines as well. Mini wearing, the second time around, didn't have the same impact. People over thirty remembered the excitement caused by the sixties girls in the first thigh length hems. The late seventies minis were of only moderate interest in comparison. Girls wore them in a less self-conscious way . Autumn styles were usually worn with dark toning tights and soft flat-heeled boots with the tops turned back just above the ankle, giving some of the wearers the look of a medieval page.

The most successful fashion of 1979 appropriately for the end of a jean wearing decade, was a new style jean. The thighs and seat were cut roomy to the point of bagginess and the legs were narrowed to the tightness of fifties drainpipes. 'Baggy jeans' were a surprisingly successful craze. After decades when tight fit had been one of the most important if not essential features in jean wearing. The looser cut was most popular with the younger generation. Boys and girls in their teens and early twenties who obviously had good figures liked the new style. Their firm shapes showed under the looser lines. The older generation carefully preserving fairly slim hips felt baggy jeans were unflattering and made them look a worse shape than they really were. An unusual situation developed; daughters and sons felt modern in baggy pants; fathers and mothers looked younger and more up to date for their age group in tight jeans.

The 1970s was a more serious decade but perhaps a better one than many people realised at the time. High living standards in the developed countries were maintained until the last few years. Even in the countries most affected by industrial problems and decline people still enjoyed far greater material wealth than in earlier decades. Parts of the world boomed and expanded throughout the seventies, in particular Japan, Hong Kong and Singapore.

Fashion was less extrovert than it had been in the sixties. However, the seventies had more

After 80 years of fashion changes, the ball dress, worn by Lady Diana Spencer, is just as glamorous, if not as fussily trimmed, as that worn in the 1900s.

than its share of changes, and far-reaching new attitudes towards clothes developed and affected the way people dressed.

Although women turned down several new fashions more confidently than they would have done in previous decades, many new lines were worn. At the beginning of the seventies clothes were narrowly fitted with very short skirts and heavy built-up shoes. By the middle of the decade looser layered garments with calf length skirts and finer shaped footwear were adopted. In 1979 broader shoulders and less bulky body lines with shorter skirts were worn with more delicately shaped shoes and boots. In 10 years trouser shapes went from tight tops and flared hems to narrow straight-legged shapes and on to full tops and narrow hems, a complete reversal of the shape of 10 years before.

Men started the seventies with side whiskers, long loose hair styles and over-fitted clothes. They ended with much shorter, neater hair and roomy athletic looking casual wear.

Both sexes wore workwear and sports inspired clothes more frequently for daily life than ever before. Formal clothes became occasion clothes. Beautiful evening dresses were created by talented designers but only worn by the very few. Tailored clothes still found a place in most women's wardrobes but younger women tended to wear them as useful all-purpose garments. The neat suit, carefully accessorised, became the older woman's style. Many men still wore conventional suits as their business uniform but they teamed them with less formal shirts and footwear.

The 1980s was greeted with less optimism than any decade since the fifties. The problems of post-war recovery and the fears of the Cold War in 1949 had made the prospects for the new decade seem very doubtful. At the end of the seventies world inflation unhappily coupled with world recession together with worries over international relations between countries, made the outlook for the new decade equally daunting. Restrained fashions reflected the mood at the end of 1949 and 1979. The fifties turned out very much better than expected and fashion got decidedly livelier; hopefully a parallel development will take place during the eighties.

Fashion has come a long way in eighty years, within some people's lifetimes. Fashion in 1980 hardly means the same thing as it did in 1900. The prosperous woman at the beginning of the century, corseted and wearing more undergarments than later generations wore for complete outfits, would have been appalled to see young women in T-shirts with slogans advertised across the front and jeans with the maker's name clearly written on the back. She would have been decidedly nervous of women dressed like young revolutionary men in baggy khaki jackets and military style trousers tucked into boots, or leather trousers and blouson tops.

The sexes would certainly look much more alike; she might even find difficulty in distinguishing between the two. Class distinction through dress would be much harder for her to discern. Armies of jeans and denim would seem drab and uniformly conformist.

The free, easy fitting shapes and the functional aspect of clothes for a much more mobile life; the selection of casual jackets, knitted garments and the wide variety of colours and designs used for footwear, all set amongst a sea of different coloured cars, would be bound to impress someone from a sedate age of horses and carriages. Athletic young people dressed and participating in active sports; tennis clothes, jogging outfits, ski wear, and wet suits for water sports, would all look awe-inspiringly futuristic.

If by some some chance a woman of the 1900s only glimpse into the future had been a ballroom in 1980, and a formal dance, what she saw would be reassuring. The music and dancing might seem odd and the hair styles of some of the young men and women strangely alike, but the girls' dresses in pale and deep coloured taffeta with tight bodices and full swirling skirts, although rather lacking in surface decoration, would look charmingly simple and unalarming.

INDEX

ACKNOWLEDGEMENTS

Laura Ashley: 205 (*left*). BBC Hulton Picture Library: 16 (*top right* and *bottom*), 17 (*left*), 21, 24, 25 (*top right*), 28, 29 (*top left*), 64 (*bottom*), 109, 111, 113, 115 (*top*), 116, 117 (*left*), 123 (*bottom*), 128, 125, 126 (*left*), 129 (*left*), 133, 136, 137, 139 (*bottom*), 141, 142, 145, 146, 147, 150, 154 (*left*), 161 (*left*). Camera Press: 173 (*left*), 179 (*right*), 182 (*right*), 187, 189, 202 (*bottom*), 214. Cinema Bookshop: 93 (*top left*), 100, 119 (*right* and *bottom left*), 122 (*left*), 149 (*top right*), 156 (*right*), 157. Daily Telegraph Colour Library: 175. Bob Gothard for Preview Magazine: 208. Illustrated London News: 16 (*top left*), 17 (*right*), 57 (*right*). Mary Evans Picture Library: 10, 22 (*top*), 23, 27, 39, 47, 50 (*left*), 62, 66, 70. Miss Selfridge: 201, 207, 215. Popperfoto: 44 (*top*), 45 (*left*), 51 (*right*), 64 (*top left*), 73 (*bottom left*), 85, 93 (*right* and *bottom left*), 110 (*left*), 118, 122 (*right*), 123 (*top left* and *right*), 149 (*top left* and *bottom*), 165 (*top left* and *right*), 167, 169, 173 (*right*), 177, 178, 180, 181, 184, 185, 193, 202 (*right*), 205 (*right*), 217 (*left*). Mary Quant: 172. The Sunday Times, John Naar: 202 (*top left*). Syndication International: 219.

JACKET
Front Cover:- *Bottom left* - The Kobal Collection; *Bottom right* - The Sunday Times, John Naar. Back Cover: *bottom* - Peter Dyer Photographs Limited.